PIAGET'S THEORY OF
COGNITIVE DEVELOPMENT

PIAGET'S THEORY OF COGNITIVE DEVELOPMENT

An Introduction
for Students of Psychology and Education

by
BARRY J. WADSWORTH
Mount Holyoke College

DAVID McKAY COMPANY, INC.
NEW YORK

PIAGET'S THEORY OF COGNITIVE DEVELOPMENT
An Introduction for Students of Psychology and Education

COPYRIGHT © 1971 BY DAVID MCKAY COMPANY, INC.

FIFTH PRINTING, JUNE 1974

ISBN:0-679-30163-1

LIBRARY OF CONGRESS CATALOG CARD NUMBER: 73-151157

MANUFACTURED IN THE UNITED STATES OF AMERICA

COVER DESIGN BY ANGELA FOOTE

To Barn at his first birthday,
Eva who has helped us both,
and my mother and father

Preface

The purpose of this book, as envisioned by the author, is to introduce the education or psychology undergraduate student to the basic concepts of Jean Piaget's theory of cognitive development. The writings of Piaget are extremely relevant to both education and psychology, but to the student not familiar with Piaget's concepts and vocabulary, reading his works is a monumental task. Most of Piaget's writings were first published in French and have undergone translation into English. In addition, a complete understanding of some of Piaget's works cannot be obtained without some sophistication in mathematics, epistemology, and logic.

Jean Flavell's invaluable book, *The Developmental Psychology of Jean Piaget* (1963), ties together the multitude of writings by Piaget and his associates. It is a reference that can take the reader quickly and accurately to the essential points of Piaget's system. But, because Flavell's book is itself of necessity very sophisticated, it usually cannot be read with ease the first time around by students. To the writer it seems an overall picture of Piaget's system is necessary before the particulars can be appreciated.

The writer has attempted to present Piaget's major concepts and notions in a simplified, conceptual manner in the hope that such an initiation to Piagetian concepts and vocabulary will be adequate to allow the reader to pursue with greater initial facility Piaget's own works and the research his writings have generated. Such an approach runs the risk of some distortion and incompleteness. This book does not cover all Piaget has to say. The emphasis has been placed on cognitive development as it relates to education and learning.

It is hoped that those reading this work will find Piaget's concepts (as construed by the writer) fascinating and appealing enough to go on to Piaget's own words where the real fruits are to be had.

Barry Wadsworth

Acknowledgments

The author wishes to thank the following publishers for their kind permission to reprint:

Basic Books from *The Construction of Reality in the Child* by Jean Piaget, translated by Margaret Cook, © 1954 by Basic Books, Inc., Publishers, New York; *The Growth of Logical Thinking from Childhood to Adolescence* by Barbel Inhelder and Jean Piaget, translated by Stanley Milfram, 1958; *The Psychology of the Child* by Jean Piaget and Barbel Inhelder, translated from the French by Helen Weaver, 1969.

Humanities Press from *Language and Thought of the Child* by Jean Piaget, 1959; *The Child's Conception of Space* by Jean Piaget and Barbel Inhelder, 1948; *Judgment and Reasoning in the Child* by Jean Piaget, 1928.

International Universities Press, Inc., from *The Origins of Intelligence in Children* by Jean Piaget, © 1953 by International Universities Press, Inc.

Random House, Inc., from *Six Psychological Studies* by Jean Piaget, edited by David Elkind, 1968. © 1967 by Random House, Inc.

Routledge and Kegan Paul Ltd. from *Language and Thought of the Child* by Jean Piaget, 1926; *Judgment and Reasoning in the Child* by Jean Piaget, 1926; *The Child's Construction of Reality* by Jean Piaget, 1955; *The Growth of Logical Thinking: From Childhood to Adolescence* by Jean Piaget and Barbel Inhelder, 1958; *The Child's Conception of Space* by Jean Piaget and Barbel Inhelder, 1967.

The Society for Research in Child Development, Inc. from Lawrence Kohlberg, "Early Education: A Cognitive-Developmental View," *Child Development*, 39 (1969).

Van Nostrand Reinhold Company from *The Developmental Psychology of Jean Piaget* by John H. Flavell, 1963, Copyright © 1963 by Litton Educational Publishing, Inc.

Contents

List of Tables

If the child partly explains the adult, it can be said that each period of his development partly explains the periods that follow.

Piaget and Inhelder, 1969, p. 3

PIAGET'S THEORY OF
COGNITIVE DEVELOPMENT

Introduction

Jean Piaget's college and university training was in the natural sciences. His main interests originally were in biology. Early in his career he became interested in children's intellectual development, and has spent the last fifty years gathering an impressive amount of research information pertaining to mental development. His work has produced an elaborate and comprehensive theory of how intelligence develops.[1] Piaget has functioned as a biologist, philosopher, logician, psychologist, and educator. In each of these fields he has made original contributions, though his contributions have had their greatest impact on psychology and education.

Piaget is thought of primarily as a child psychologist and educator in America. In the strict sense of the word, he is neither. His work is not directly concerned with predicting behavior as the psychologist's frequently is, nor is he directly concerned with how to teach children. He prefers to be classified as a genetic epistemologist.[2] His work is primarily concerned with describing and explaining in a very

---

[1] In this writing, the terms *intellectual, cognitive,* and *mental* will be used interchangeably.

[2] Genetic epistemology is a science of how knowledge is acquired.

systematic way the growth and development of intellectual structures and knowledge. Needless to say, his work has had a great impact on both education and psychology here and abroad.

Piaget's publications, all written originally in French, took many years to cross the Atlantic. Only recently have Piaget's works and concepts been spreading quickly throughout educational and psychological thought in America. L'Abate's 1968 frequency of citation study[3] is a measure of the impact of Piaget's works on American thought. His search of journals and textbooks in the child development field during the 1950s and 1960s found Piaget to be the most frequently cited author.

BIOGRAPHY

Piaget's life has been one of scholarship and hard work. He was born in 1896 in Neuchâtel, Switzerland. By his own admission, he was an intellectually precocious youth. At the age of 10, he managed his first publication, a description of a partly albino sparrow he observed in a public park. To some extent, the direction and rigor of Piaget's efforts were determined early in his life. At the age of 15, he had decided to direct his work toward a biological explanation of knowledge, a goal that is still clearly reflected in his work.

In 1915, at the age of 18, Piaget received his baccalaureate from the University of Neuchâtel in Switzerland. Three years later, he received a doctorate in the natural sciences from the same school. During this period, much of Piaget's time was spent studying the development of mollusks in

---

[3] Two journals, *Child Development* (1950-1965) and *Journal of Genetic Psychology* (1957-8, 1960-5) were searched, along with twelve popular and current textbooks on child development.

the many lakes around Neuchâtel. By the age of 21, he had published twenty-five professional papers (mostly on mollusks), and was considered one of the world's few experts on mollusks.

His intensive work in biology led him to conclude that biological development was due not only to maturation (and heredity) but also to variables in the environment. He observed in successive generations of mollusks certain structural changes that could only be attributed to movement from large lakes with much wave action to small ponds. Such observations convinced Piaget that biological development was a process of adaptation to the environment; that it could not be explained by maturation alone (Piaget, "Autobiography," 1952, p. 250). Experiences and convictions such as these contributed to Piaget's later view of mental development as being primarily a process of adaptation to the environment and an extension of biological development.

After completing his doctorate, Piaget's primary interest turned to psychology. For several years he had been reading books on and taking classes in psychology, and he had become increasingly interested in the field. He went to Zurich in 1918 and studied and worked in several psychological clinics, deciding to immerse himself in psychological experimentation. In 1919 he went to Paris and spent two years at the Sorbonne. While in Paris, Piaget had a chance to work in Binet's[4] laboratory (a grade school) standardizing several tests. Unenthusiastic at first, he became intrigued with the incorrect answers children gave to questions on the tests, and shortly thereafter, he was hard at work examining the reasoning processes underlying

---

[4] Binet is considered father of the Binet Intelligence Test from which the current forms of the Stanford-Binet were derived.

children's responses. Piaget had found his research interest. For two years he continued testing children, examining the development of their thought. This was the beginning of Piaget's experimental activity in psychology.

In 1921 Piaget was offered the position of director of studies at the Institut J. J. Rousseau in Geneva (Ibid., p. 245), a position that proved to be the perfect environment for the studies he was interested in. He accepted the position and was launched on a course of research that has not changed since: the investigation of the mental development of children.

By the age of 30, Piaget was famous for his initial works in psychology.[5] Through the years he has conducted a continuous research, and he has taught at the University of Geneva. A prolific writer, he has published over thirty books and hundreds of journal articles, several in conjunction with the colleagues he has assembled in Geneva. He attributes much of his own productivity to the group of co-workers that have worked with him over the years.

Piaget is reported to be an untiring worker, at 73 still following a strenuous daily self-imposed work schedule. Each summer, at the school year's end, he is reported (Elkind, 1968) to collect his research findings for the year and head for an abandoned farmhouse in the Alps where he spends the summer in isolation, writing and walking, his whereabouts unknown to but a few friends and his family. When the summer ends, Piaget returns from the mountains—with a new book or two—and several articles (Elkind, 1968).

Piaget has been honored around the world. He holds

---

[5] *The Language and Thought of the Child* (1924) and *Judgment and Reasoning of the Child* (1924) were Piaget's first books published in psychology, though he had published numerous papers in the field prior to these publications.

honorary degrees from Harvard (1936), Columbia (1970), the University of Brussels (1949), the Sorbonne (1946), and Brazil (1949). In recent years he has made several trips to the United States to address American groups concerned with child development.

In 1955, with the help of a grant from the Rockefeller Foundation, the Centre International d'Epistémologie Génétique was established in Geneva. This program permits three eminent scholars a year to visit and do research with the Geneva group that has grown up around Piaget. Several Americans have studied in Geneva under this program, and to some extent, this has helped spread interest in Piaget's work. Whether Piaget's efforts and basic assumptions prove to be correct or incorrect in total or in part, his works have generated more interest and research than those of any other person in psychology in the last fifty years.

APPROACH TO RESEARCH

Piaget is a developmental psychologist in that he is concerned with uncovering the ontogenetic[6] changes in cognitive functioning from birth through adolescence. His works have been slow to gain wide attention in the United States. The reasons for this (aside from the already-mentioned fact that his works were all originally published in French) are many, but in large part these reasons are theoretical and methodological. The concepts he uses have not gained acceptance easily in the United States, nor has his "experimental" methodology.

Psychology in the United States has a strong tradition of behaviorism. Such men as Thorndike, Tolman, Watson,

---

[6] Ontogenetic: those developmental changes that occur in the individual.

Hull, Spence, and Skinner have dominated the scene, each of them primarily interested in stimulus-response relationships and the concept of reinforcement. Traditionally, American psychologists of the behaviorist school do not infer the existence of internal mental processes (of thought). Piaget's concepts like assimilation are entirely foreign to the behaviorist position. He does not conceptualize behavior in terms of stimuli and responses, nor does he use the construct of reinforcement. Some of Piaget's concepts are assimilation, accommodation, equilibrium, and schemata. Also, he does infer the existence of internal mental processes. Consequently, it has been difficult for American psychologists to come to grips with Piaget's concepts.

In America, experimental research in psychology has typically concerned itself with hypothesis testing, rigorous control of experimental variables, and treatment of data with sophisticated statistical procedures. Most of Piaget's research has not been experimental, nor does he frequently employ elaborate statistics and test hypotheses. From his work in Paris in Binet's clinic, Piaget evolved a clinical-descriptive technique that came to serve as a trademark for his work. It essentially involved asking individual children carefully selected questions and noting their responses. In other cases, data were nothing more than the observation of infant behavior. These techniques could hardly be called experimental in the restricted sense of the word, though they were invariably systematic and his analyses were exceedingly detailed: designed to detect developmental changes in cognitive functioning.

Piaget frequently permitted himself to be led by his "intuition" when interviewing children, particularly in his earlier works. In the clinical approach, any two children are not necessarily asked the same questions in the same setting. In effect, no two children ever receive the same experimental treatment. *The Child's Conception of the World* (1929) is an example of Piaget's skillful selection of questions. The book is without statistical tables, and "sample sizes" are small. The main sources for three of Piaget's books were observations of his own three children, born between 1925 and 1931.[7] These meticulous observations provided him with an awareness of the relationship between early sensorimotor actions and later cognitive development. From these exceedingly complete and careful descriptions of behavior over a period of years, major conclusions have been drawn regarding intellectual development from birth to age 2. This type of research has been criticized severely by some because of the small "sample size," and because it is not experimental. The criticisms diminish in importance if one accepts the assumption implicit in Piaget's theory: that the general course of development of intellectual structures is the same in all persons. If this is true, then sample sizes can become meaningless. It should also be stated that there is much merit in using the longitudinal approach that Piaget has used. While frequently observing small numbers of children, his observations of the same subjects have on occasion ranged over years.

While much of Piaget's early work can be looked upon as intuitive, employing nonexperimental procedures and using small samples of subjects, a large part of his more recent work is as rigorously experimental as any psychologist might wish. *The Early Growth of Logic in the Child* (1964) and *The Mechanisms of Perception* (1969) carefully report statistical findings and respectable sample

---

[7] *Play, Dreams, and Imitation in Childhood* (1951), *The Origins of Intelligence in Children* (1952).

sizes. The material reported in *The Growth of Logical Thinking from Childhood to Adolescence* (1958) is based on the testing of over 1500 subjects.

While many criticisms have been leveled at Piaget's approach to research, none has disputed that it is always systematic, rigorous, and insightful. Piaget's primary technique has been one of systematic observation, description, and analysis of children's behavior. This approach is primarily designed to discover the nature and level of development of the concepts children use, not to produce developmental scales. Piaget defends the approach he has taken to research on the basis that it is the most appropriate for the questions he seeks to answer. While this is very reasonable, it does not always rest well with one who has sanctified American experimental procedures.

THE ORGANIZATION OF THE BOOK

One of the difficulties encountered by the uninitiated in reading Piaget's works is a number of unique concepts he uses to conceptualize behavior. It is necessary to understand these before his works can be understood. Chapter One is a description of four of the concepts that are central to all Piaget's work: schema, assimilation, accommodation, and equilibrium. Chapter Two deals with the relationship between cognitive development and factors such as heredity, action, motivation, and stages of development.

Each of Chapters Three through Six deals with one of the four stages of cognitive development, in the order in which they occur. Chapter Seven discusses the relationship of cognitive development to adolescent behavior. The final chapter summarizes the previous chapters and discusses some of the implications of Piaget's works for child training and education.

Chapter One

Intellectual Organization and Adaptation

Piaget's system for conceptualizing cognitive development has been greatly influenced by his early training and work as a biologist. Functioning as a biologist, he became vividly aware of and impressed by the interaction of mollusks with their environment. Mollusks, like all living organisms, are constantly adapting to changes in environmental conditions.

From this early work, Piaget came to believe that biological acts are acts of *adaptation* to the physical environment and *organizations* of the environment. This led him to conceptualize intellectual development in much the same way. Cognitive acts are seen as acts of *organization* of and *adaptation* to the perceived environment. This is not to imply in any sense that mental behavior can be attributed to biological functioning, but that the concepts of biological development are useful and valid for looking at intellectual development. Indeed, Piaget asserts (*The Origins of Intelligence in Children*, 1952) that the basic principles of cognitive development are the *same* as those of biological development.

Organization and adaptation are not viewed by Piaget as separate processes. He writes:

9

From the biological point of view organization is inseparable from adaptation: They are two complementary processes of a single mechanism, the first being the internal aspect of the cycle of which adaptation constitutes the external aspect [Piaget, Ibid., p. 7].

For Piaget, intellectual activity cannot be separated from the "total" functioning of the organism. Thus, he considers intellectual functioning as a special form of biological activity (Ibid., p. 42). Intellectual and biological activity are both part of the overall process by which an organism adapts to the environment and organizes experience.

To understand the processes of intellectual organization and adaptation as they are viewed by Piaget, four basic concepts are required. These are the concepts of *schema*, *assimilation*, *accommodation*, and *equilibrium*. These concepts are used to explain how and why mental development occurs. They are discussed in that order.

SCHEMA

Piaget believed the mind had to have structures much in the same way the body does. All animals have a stomach, a structure that permits eating and digestion. To help explain why children (all persons) make rather stable responses to stimuli, and to account for many of the phenomena associated with memory, Piaget used the word schema. Schemata are the cognitive *structures* by which individuals intellectually adapt to and organize the environment. *Schemata* are structures that are the mental counterparts of biological means of adapting. The stomach is a biological structure that animals use successfully to adapt to their environment. In much the same way, schemata are equivalent structures that adapt and change with mental development. These structures are inferred to exist.

They are constructs in the same way that Freud's Id and Ego are.

Schemata can be simplistically thought of as concepts or categories. Another analogy might be an index file in which each index card represents a schema. Adults have many cards or schemata. They are used to process and identify incoming stimuli. In this way the organism is able to differentiate between stimulus events and to generalize. When a child is born, it has few schemata (cards on file). As the child develops, his schemata gradually broaden (become more generalized), become more differentiated, and progressively more "adult." Schemata never stop changing or becoming more refined. Indeed, the sensori-motor schemata of childhood develop into the schemata of adulthood. So we have a picture of an index card file in the child's head. At birth it contains only a few large cards on which everything is written. As the child develops, more cards are necessary to contain the changing classifications. As an illustration, imagine a child walking down a country road with his parents. The child looks into a field and sees what is conventionally called a cow. The child says, "Look at the big dog!" What does the child's response mean in terms of intellectual functioning? Assuming the child made an honest response, we could infer something like this: The child looked out into the field and saw a cow. Presented with this "new" stimulus (he never saw a cow before), the child tried to place the stimulus in reference to a card in his card file. In terms of the things the child could identify, the stimulus (cow) most closely approximated a dog, so the child identified the object as a dog (a schema or file).

In Piaget's terms, we would say that the child has a number of schemata. These schemata are analogous to concepts, categories, or cards in a file. When confronted with a stimulus, the child tried to "fit" the stimulus into an available schema. Thus the child quite logically called the cow a dog, since the cow closely approximated a dog, and met all the child's criteria for what a dog was. The child was not able to perceive the differences between a cow and a dog, but he was able to see the similarities.

Schemata are intellectual structures that organize events as they are perceived by the organism into groups according to common characteristics. They are repeatable psychological events in the sense that the child will repeatedly classify stimuli in a consistent manner. If the child "consistently" classifies cows as dogs, we can infer something about the nature of the child's concepts (schemata of cows and dogs).

At birth, schemata are reflexive in nature. That is, they can be inferred from simple reflex motor activities such as sucking, grasping, and so on. The sucking reflex illustrates a reflexive schema. At birth, infants typically will suck on whatever is put in their mouths—a nipple, a finger—suggesting that there is no differentiation, or that only a single, global sucking schema exists. Shortly after birth, infants learn to differentiate: milk-producing stimuli are accepted and non milk-producing stimuli are rejected. At this point, a differentiation exists, or in Piaget's words, the infant has two sucking schemata, one for milk-producing stimuli and one for non milk-producing stimuli. At this time, schemata are not yet "mental" in the sense in which we usually think of the term. Schemata are reflexive. The infant makes real differentiations within his limited environment, but they are made via the reflexive and motor apparatus he has available. These differentiations on the most primitive level are the precursors of later "mental" activities. As the child develops, schemata become more differentiated, less sensory, more numerous, and the network they form becomes increasingly more complex. During early childhood, an infant has a few reflexive schemata that allow him to make very few differentiations in the environment. An adult has a vast array of comparatively complex schemata that permit a great number of differentiations. The schemata of the adult evolve from the schemata of the child through adaptation and organization.

It would be misleading to think that schemata do not change, or that the child is destined to call cows dogs for the rest of his days. Obviously, this does not happen. As the child becomes better able to differentiate between stimuli, schemata become more numerous (differentiated). As he becomes better able to generalize across stimuli, schemata become more refined.

At any point in time, a child's responses are assumed to reflect the nature of the child's concepts or schemata at that time. It is entirely "logical" for the child described in the example to call a cow a dog when the schemata he has available are considered. Schemata are defined by (or reflected in) the overt behavior of the child. But schemata are more than the behavior; they are the structure from which the behaviors flow. Behavior patterns that occur repeatedly in the course of cognitive activity are conceptualized as reflecting schemata. A schema subsumes a whole collection of distinct but similar action sequences. "Every schema is . . . coordinated with all other schemata and itself constitutes a totality with differentiated parts [Piaget, *The Origins of Intelligence in Children*, 1952, p. 7]."

Since schemata are structures of cognitive development that do change, allowance must be made for their growth and development. Adults have different concepts from children.   Concepts (schemata—their structural counter-parts) change. The cognitive schemata of the adult are de-rived from the sensori-motor schema of the child. The pro-cesses responsible for the change are *assimilation* and *accommodation*.

ASSIMILATION

Assimilation is the cognitive *process* by which the person integrates new perceptual matter or stimulus events into existing schemata or patterns of behavior. One might say that the child has experiences: It sees new things (cows) or sees old things in new ways, and hears things. What the child tries to do is to fit these new events or stimuli into the schemata he has at the time.[1] Suppose, as in the pre-

---

[1] Assimilation is a term Piaget borrowed from biology. It is the cognitive counterpart of eating, wherein food is eaten, digested, and assimilated or changed into a usable form.

vious example, a child is walking down the country road with his father, and the father points to a cow in the field and says, "What is that?" The child looks at the cow (stimulus) and says, "That's a dog." What has happened? The child, seeing the object in the field (cow), sifted through his collection of schemata until he found one that seemed appropriate and that could include the object. To the child, the object (cow) had all the characteristics of a dog—it fit in his dog schema—so the child concluded that the object was a dog. The stimulus (cow) was assimilated into the dog schema. Thus assimilation can be viewed as the cognitive process of placing new stimulus events into existing schemata.

Assimilation goes on all the time. It would be extreme oversimplification to suggest that a person processes one stimulus at a time. The human must continually process an increasing number of stimuli.

Assimilation theoretically does not result in the development (change) of schemata, but does affect their growth. One might compare a schema to a balloon, and assimilation to putting more air in the balloon. The balloon gets larger (assimilation growth) but does not change its shape (development). Assimilation is a part of the process by which the individual cognitively adapts to and organizes the environment. The process of assimilation allows for growth of schemata. This does not account for change (development) of schemata. We know schemata change—adult schemata are different from children's. Piaget accounts for the change of schemata with *accommodation.*

③ ACCOMMODATION

Upon being confronted with a new stimulus, the child tries to assimilate it into existing schemata. Sometimes this is not possible. Sometimes a stimulus cannot be placed or assimilated into a schema because there are no schemata into which it fits. The characteristics of the stimulus do not approximate those required in any of the child's available schemata. What does the child do? Essentially he can do one of two things: He can create a new schema into which he can place the stimulus, or he can modify an existing schema so that the stimulus will fit into it; both of these are forms of *accommodation*. Thus, accommodation is the creation of new schemata or the modification of old schemata. Both of these actions result in a change in or development of cognitive structures (schemata).

Once accommodation has taken place, the child can try again to assimilate the stimulus. Since the structure has changed, the stimulus is readily assimilated. Assimilation is always the end-product that the child actively seeks.

The child who is actively assimilating and accommodating is in no way required or expected to evolve schemata that assume a particular form. Implicit in the conceptualizations of schema used here is the idea that schemata develop over time with experience. At first, while the child is an infant, they are very global—and when compared to adults, extremely imprecise and frequently inaccurate. The processes of assimilation and accommodation that convert infants' rather inaccurate schemata into the more useful adult-like schemata obviously take years.

Another word about assimilation and accommodation. It can be seen that in assimilation, the person imposes his available structure on the stimuli being processed. That is, the stimuli are "forced" to fit the person's structure. In accommodation, the reverse is true. The person is "forced" to change his schema to fit the new stimuli. Accommodation accounts for development (a qualitative change), and assimilation accounts for growth (a quantitative change); together they account for intellectual adaptation and the development of intellectual structures.

SOMETIMES YOU JUST HAVE TO ACCOMMODATE !

 EQUILIBRIUM

The processes of assimilation and accommodation are necessary for cognitive growth and development. Of equal importance are the relative amounts of assimilation and accommodation that take place. For example, imagine the logical outcome in terms of mental development if a person always assimilated stimuli and never accommodated. Such a person would end up with a few very large schemata and be unable to detect differences in things. On the other hand, what would be the result if the person always accommodated, and never assimilated? This would result in a person having a great number of very small schemata that would have little generality. The person would be unable to detect similarities. Either of these extremes would be disastrous. Thus it can be seen that a "balance" between assimilation and accommodation is as necessary as the processes themselves. The "balance" between assimilation and accommodation is referred to by

Piaget as *equilibrium*. It is necessary to ensure an efficient interaction of the developing child with the environment.

Equilibrium is a balance between assimilation and accommodation. *Disequilibrium* is an imbalance between assimilation and accommodation. When disequilibrium occurs, cognitively, it provides motivation for the child to seek equilibrium—to further assimilate or accommodate. Equilibrium is seen as a necessary condition toward which the organism constantly strives. The organism ultimately assimilates all stimuli (or stimulus events) with or without accommodation. This results in equilibrium. Thus, equilibrium can be viewed as a state of cognitive "balance" that is reached at assimilation. Obviously, equilibrium relevant to any particular stimulus may be a very temporary affair, but it is nonetheless important.

Everything must be assimilated by the child. The schemata the child uses may not be in harmony with those of adults (like classifying a cow as a dog), but the child's organization will *always* be internally consistent. The child's placement of stimuli into schemata is theoretically always appropriate for his level of conceptual development. There is no "wrong" placement. There are just better and better placements.

We can say, then, that the child, upon experiencing a new stimulus (or an old one again), tries to assimilate the stimulus into an existing schema. If he is successful, equilibrium is attained for the moment, relevant to the particular stimulus event. If the child cannot assimilate the stimulus, he then attempts to accommodate by modifying a schema or creating a new one. When this is done, assimilation of the stimulus proceeds and equilibrium is reached.

Conceptually, cognitive growth and development proceeds in this way at *all* levels of development, from birth

Where can I put this?   Ah.. ha..!   Love that equilibrium!

through adulthood, the schemata of the adult being built from the schemata of the child. It is important to note that in assimilation, the organism "fits" stimuli into schemata that exist, while in accommodation the organism "changes" schemata to fit the stimulus. It can be seen that the process of accommodation results in a qualitative change in intellectual structures (schemata) while assimilation only adds to the existing structures—a quantitative change. Thus it is that assimilation and accommodation, a cumulative coordination and integration, account for the growth and development of cognitive structures.

Chapter Two

Cognitive Development and Other Factors

HEREDITY AND COGNITIVE DEVELOPMENT

Piaget (*The Origins of Intelligence in Children*, 1952) subscribes to the importance of heredity in all development, both biological and intellectual. He asserts that to some degree inherited neurological structures impede or facilitate intellectual functioning, but that they cannot account for intellectual functioning by themselves (Ibid., pp. 1-3). Inherited neurological structures influence cognitive development, but the structure alone cannot explain the development. Piaget asserts that properties other than neurological structures are inherited that affect cognitive development, in part account for individual differences, and make intellectual progress possible. These properties are called *functional invariants*.

The functional invariants are essentially the processes of assimilation and accommodation that permit cognitive organization and adaptation. These functional invariants can be thought of as combining to produce *a mode of intellectual functioning*—the particular way in which a particular organism adapts to and organizes the environment. An individual could be one who tends to assimilate more than he accommodates. Variations in the relative amounts of assimilation and accommodation can be thought of as a

20

mode of functioning. The mode remains fixed (invariant) throughout the course of one's life, each individual having a unique, genetically determined mode. According to Piaget, in cognitive development, development that is environmentally, as well as genetically determined, biological endowment plays a role, but *does not* predetermine intellectual functioning at any given point in life. The functioning and structures that develop after birth are determined by the interaction of the inherited properties and the environment (experience). Thus neither experience alone nor endowment alone can determine cognitive development.

CONTENT, FUNCTION, AND STRUCTURE

Intelligence is viewed by Piaget as having three components: content, function, and structure. *Content* refers to observable behaviors—sensori-motor and conceptual—that reflect intellectual activity. The content of intelligence, because of its nature, varies considerably from age to age and from child to child. *Function* refers to those characteristics of intellectual activity—assimilation and accommodation—that are stable and continual throughout cognitive development. *Structure* refers to the inferred organizational properties (schemata) that explain the occurrence of particular behaviors. If a child is asked to compare a row of 9 checkers to a longer row of 8 checkers and determine which has more checkers, and the child says the row of 8 checkers has more, even though he counts each row, one can infer that the child does not have a complete concept of number. This would suggest that his schema for number is not yet fully developed. When confronted with a problem that pits perception against *reason*, his choice is based on perception. Eventually *reason* will prevail, but only after the determining structures have changed. These changes in *structures* are intellectual development. Flavell (1963) writes:

> Interposed between function and content, Piaget postulates the existence of cognitive structures. Structure, like content and unlike function, does indeed change with age, and these developmental changes constitute the major object of study for Piaget. What are the structures in Piaget's system? They are the organizational properties of intelligence (schémata), organizations created through function and inferrable from the behavioral content whose nature they determine [p. 17].

Piaget has concerned himself primarily with the structure of intelligence, though he does deal with function and content to a lesser degree. His work involves the careful description and analysis of *qualitative* changes in development of these cognitive structures (schemata). Presumably, qualitative structural changes in cognitive functioning most clearly are changes in intellectual functioning—what is commonly called intelligence.[1]

STRUCTURE AND CONTENT CHANGE – FUNCTION DOES NOT

ACTION AND COGNITIVE DEVELOPMENT

Piaget's system requires that the child *act* in the environment if cognitive development is to proceed. The develop-

---

[1] It should be noted that most "intelligence" tests to a large extent sample cognitive content, not cognitive structure. By and large, they are quantitative measures, not qualitative. Piaget's conceptualizations suggest that "intelligence" tests should measure cognitive structures if development is to be accurately assessed.

ment of cognitive structures is ensured only if the child assimilates and accommodates stimuli in the environment. This can only come about if the child's senses are brought to bear on the environment. When the child is acting in the environment, moving in space, manipulating objects, searching with his eyes and ears, he is taking in the raw ingredients to be assimilated and accommodated. These actions result in the development of schemata. An infant cannot learn to differentiate between a nipple and an edge of his blanket unless he *acts* on them both.

As the child becomes older, actions resulting in cognitive change become less overt. For the infant, the instrumental act may be movement of the arm and grasping. For the 9-year-old the instrumental act may be an internal one, as in adding a column of numbers. In both cases the *activity* of the child is essential for development.

Actions in the environment are a necessary but not sufficient condition for cognitive development. That is, the experience alone does not ensure development, but development cannot take place without it. Also necessary for development are the functional invariants, assimilation and accommodation, whose functional relationship is thought to be in part an innate or inherited (biologically linked) characteristic. Thus there are several interacting determinants of cognitive development, one of which is action.

The child is more dependent on physical and sensorial experience in the earlier years of life when he does not possess the power of symbolic representation (language). At this time, interaction with the environment is completely on a sensory and motor level. The child acts directly on objects in the environment. Development proceeds as the infant explores his environment via his reflexes. A variety of objects are placed in the mouth or sucked via the sucking reflex. Objects are grasped. These active reflexive behaviors allow the infant to make his first differentiations of the environment. These acts allow the child to develop internal sensori-motor representations (schemata) of the objects as he makes discriminations.

At a later age, the child's actions on the environment will be mediated by internalized symbols and language and will be less overt. Actions will be less sensori-motor and more conceptual. Nonetheless, the active participation of the child remains necessary for cognitive development. The child learning to add a column of figures is acting on the environment. The behavior is covert, but nonetheless an action.

MOTIVATION

Piaget has not dealt extensively with the question of motivation of cognitive behavior: what energizes behavior and provides the direction for behavior. He rejects the notion of extrinsic "needs" (external forces) as being responsible for motivating cognitive behavior in the organism. In doing this, he rejects the concept of reinforcement that is central to behaviorism and learning theory. The "need" to engage in cognitive activity is, according to Piaget, an intrinsic need—motivation is from within the organism, not from without. This comes about, Piaget says, because cognitive structures, once developed and functioning, perpetuate themselves by more functioning. In the acts of assimilation and accommodation, there is an intrinsic tendency to assimilate and accommodate the environment. Piaget writes (*The Origins of Intelligence in Children*, 1952, pp. 45-46):

> . . . in the young child the principal needs are of a functional category. The functioning of the organs engenders, through its very existence . . . a series of vicarious needs whose com-

plexity transcends, from the very beginning, simple organic satisfaction (primary needs) . . . the principal motive power of intellectual activity thus becoming the need to incorporate things into the subject's schemata . . . the basic fact is not need of such but rather the act of assimilation.

The primary motivating force for cognitive activity is the process of assimilation, which, once developed, by its very nature seeks out the environment. The nature of the mechanisms of assimilation and accommodation is to function, and the need to function cannot be separated from the functioning itself. Thus, motivation, according to Piaget, is intrinsic in the organism.

PERIODS OF DEVELOPMENT

In the broadest sense, Piaget asserts throughout his work that cognitive and intellectual changes are the result of a developmental process. Piaget's general "hypothesis" is simply that cognitive development is a coherent process of successive qualitative changes of cognitive structures (schemata), each structure and its concommitant change deriving logically and inevitably from the preceding one. Successive schemata do not replace prior ones; they incorporate them, resulting in a qualitative change. If the young boy who classified a cow as a dog suddenly at some later time decides that the cow is no longer a dog, but a new object called a "cow," he does not *replace* schemata. What he may do is create a new schema (accommodate) for cow-like objects, while retaining his old schema for dogs. Thus a change has occurred that results in a qualitatively superior set of schemata, the current schemata incorporating the previous ones.

For purposes of conceptualizing cognitive growth, intellectual development can be divided into four broad periods (and other subperiods, stages, and substages).[2] Piaget has been criticized for the use of periods or stages in his theory. Those who object to his use of stages *probably* do so out of misunderstanding. Piaget does not suggest that children move from discrete stage to discrete stage in development, as one moves from one step to another while walking upstairs. Cognitive development flows along, but the stages are useful to the observer conceptualizing the developmental process. The researcher and theorist can divide the long period of development into periods of shorter length, and in that way development can be analyzed and, in some ways, conceptualized more efficiently. This does not in any way deny the continuity of development over its entire course, nor does it mean that the periods are selected without a rationale.

Piaget (*The Psychology of Intelligence*, 1963) broadly summarizes the periods (or stages) of cognitive development as:

1. *The period of sensori-motor intelligence (0-2 years).* During this period behavior is primarily motor. The child does not yet "think" conceptually, though "cognitive" development is seen.

2. *The period of preoperational thought (2-7 years).* This period is characterized by the development of language and rapid conceptual development.

3. *The period of concrete operations (7-11 years).* During these years the child develops the ability to apply logical thought to *concrete* problems.

---

[2] The number of stages one divides development into is somewhat arbitrary. Piaget has on different occasions divided development into three, four, or six major stages, each time with a number of substages. The author has, for his purposes, divided development into four stages.

4. *The period of formal operations (11-15 years).* During this period the child's cognitive *structures* reach their greatest level of development, and the child becomes able to apply logic to all classes of problems.

Development is thought to flow along in a cumulative manner, each new step in development becoming integrated with previous steps. The behaviors described are only typical behaviors of a given age, period, or stage. Piaget writes (*The Origins of Intelligence in Children*, 1952, p. 329):

> In a general way, the fact should be emphasized that the behavior patterns characteristic of the different stages do not succeed each other in a linear way (those of a given stage disappearing at the time when those of the following one take form) but in the manner of the layers of a pyramid (upright, or upside down), the new behavior patterns simply being added to the old ones to complete, correct, or combine with them.

It should be mentioned again that the stages are not independent stages in actual development. Also, the chronological ages during which children can be expected to develop behavior representative of a particular stage are not fixed. The age spans that have been suggested by Piaget are *normative* and only suggest the times during which most children can be expected to display the intellectual behaviors that are characteristic of the particular stage. This in no way means that children cannot display some aspects of preoperational thought at age 1, or still be displaying some aspects of preoperational thought at age 10. The behaviors that will be described for each stage are *only* typical for the age groups. The norms that have been established by Piaget are for samples of children in Geneva, and do not necessarily hold for American samples. Piaget assumes that the fixed order of appearance (of structures of behavior) implies nothing concerning the experiential or hereditary basis for the order. The age at which the stages occur can vary with the nature of both the individual's experience and his hereditary potential (Ibid., p. 255). Progress through stages is not automatic (as in maturation theory).

One aspect of the stage theory of Piaget is "fixed." According to Piaget, every child *must* pass through the stages of cognitive development in the same order. A child cannot move intellectually from the preoperational stage to the period of formal operations without passing through the period of concrete operations.

While this is true, the rates at which children pass through the stages may not be identical, due to experiential or hereditary factors. "Bright" children may go through the stages rapidly; "dull" children more slowly, some never reaching or completing the last stages (formal operations).

While a concept of stages of intellectual development is used, it should be remembered that the range of intellectual behaviors within a particular stage is quite large. That is, while the child develops the use of symbolic representation (language) during the preoperational period (2 to 7 years), it is expected that language usage at age 7 will be qualitatively different than at age 2.

In the early part of the preoperational stage, language ability is being formed and organized. Thus, the language behaviors of the 3-year-old typically lack the organization and stability of the 7-year-old, though they will both demonstrate characteristics of the stage. Thus it is that behaviors early in a stage, or early in the development of a particular intellectual function, can be expected to have less stability and to be less sophisticated than in later periods.

PERIOD TRANSITION FACTORS

So far it has been made clear that, according to Piaget, cognitive development follows a "fixed" course wherein the child moves progressively through four major stages. From birth through adulthood the structures of intelligence, schemata, are constantly developing as the child acts on the environment and assimilates and accommodates to an increasing array of stimuli in his environment. Are there other factors that act to influence the course of cognitive development? According to Piaget, there are.

Piaget (1961) suggests there are four broad factors that are related to all cognitive development: (1) maturation, (2) physical experience, (3) social interaction, and (4) a general progression of equilibrium (Ibid., p. 277). Piaget views each of these factors and their interaction as necessary conditions for cognitive development, but none of them, by themselves, is seen as sufficient to ensure cognitive development. Movement within and between stages of development is a function of these factors and their actions.

Maturation

For Piaget, maturation is a factor in cognitive development. The main contribution of maturation to cognitive development is in neurological growth (the growth of brain tissue) and the development of the endocrine system (Piaget, 1969). While maturation clearly plays a part in development, its importance is somewhat minimized by Piaget:

> The maturation of the nervous system can do no more than determine the totality of possibilities and impossibilities at a given stage. A particular social environment remains indispens-

able for the realization of these possibilities. It follows that their realization can be accelerated or retarded as a function of cultural or educational conditions [Inhelder and Piaget, 1958, p. 337].

Physical Experience

A second factor in cognitive development is physical experience. The child must have experience with objects and stimuli in the environment in which he acts on objects. Assimilation and accommodation cannot take place unless there is interaction between the organism and the environment. Not only must the child have experience, but he must act on the environment, not just react to it (as in S-R learning theory). The growth of cognitive structures (schemata) via assimilation and accommodation requires that the child interact with the environment. Early in life, interaction with the environment is primarily on a sensorimotor level. The child manipulates the environment in a direct manner. The hand grasps objects; the mouth sucks objects, the eyes explore. As the child develops, interaction with the environment becomes increasingly symbolic in nature. The child reads, counts, speaks. To the extent that the child actively assimilates and accommodates to the environment, he will develop cognitively. Schemata cannot develop unless they are fed stimuli that invoke assimilation and accommodation.

Social Interaction

Another factor in cognitive development is social interaction. By social interaction, Piaget means the interchange of ideas between people. This is particularly important. The concepts or schemata that people develop can be classified as two types: those that have sensorially available physical referents (they can be seen, heard, and so on), and those that do not have such referents. The concept "tree" has physical referents; the concept "honesty" does not. A child can develop a socially acceptable concept of "tree" relatively independent of others, for referents are usually available. But the same child cannot develop a socially acceptable concept of "honesty" independent of others. To the extent that concepts are "arbitrary" or socially defined, the child is dependent on social interaction for the construction and validation of his concepts.

Social interaction can be of many types. There is interaction with peers, parents, and other adults. The events that take place in a schoolroom are most frequently the interaction of students with other students and their teachers. There is also the interaction with parents and others in the environment. All of these are important in cognitive development.

Equilibration

The previous concepts of maturation, experience, and social interaction do not suffice to explain cognitive development. Mental behaviors are observed that suggest the child contributes an organizational, or regulating quality, to development. Piaget (1961) writes:

> ... if the development depends ... on internal factors (maturation) ... and ... on external factors (physical or social), it is self-evident that these internal and external factors equilibrate each other ... We believe ... that the mental equilibrium and even the biological one presumes an activity of the subject ... It consists in a sort of matching, oriented towards compensation ... [p. 279].

Piaget and Inhelder (1969) also say:

> An internal mechanism (though it cannot be reduced to heredity alone and has no preestablished plan, since there is in fact construction) is observable at the time of each partial construction and each transition from one stage to the next. It is a process of equilibrium . . . of self-regulation; that is, a series of active compensations on the part of the subject in response to external disturbances and an adjustment that is both retroactive (loop systems or feedback) and anticipation, constituting a permanent system of compensations [p. 157].

Thus, equilibration (attaining equilibrium) is seen as an internal self-regulating system that operates to reconcile the roles of maturation, experience, and social interaction.

SUMMARY

Heredity, according to Piaget, most influences cognitive development in that it determines the nature of the *functional invariants* (assimilation and accommodation). Development proceeds as a function of the interaction of endowment and experience. The child must act on the environment.

Intelligence is seen as having three components: content, function, and structure. Piaget has primarily studied the development of schemata, the structures of intelligence.

Motivation, according to Piaget, is an "intrinsic" force that is self-activating once assimilation and accommodation begin. Development proceeds through four major stages. It is both fixed and continuous. All persons develop through the same stages in the same way, though not necessarily at the same rates. Four factors were described as being "necessary" for transition between stages: maturation, experience, social interaction, and equilibration.

Chapter Three

The Sensori-Motor Period

Mental development is a process that begins the day the infant is born (and possibly sooner). This does not mean that the child is born thinking (internally representing objects in the mind), but it does mean that the sensori-motor behaviors that occur from birth on are necessary for and instrumental in later cognitive development. To look at it another way, intellectual behavior at any age evolves directly from prior levels of behavior. Thus the roots of all intellectual development are in early sensori-motor behavior.

Piaget has carefully described development during the first two years of life in several books. From his observations and writings, it is clear that the structures of intelligence begin to evolve during infancy. At birth, the child can perform only simple reflex behaviors. Two years later he is typically beginning to talk (symbolic representation), and he has clearly evolved intellectual operations. The child can solve most sensori-motor problems, i.e., he can get objects he wants; he can use one object to retrieve another; he can mentally "invent" means (behaviors) that will permit him to do things he wants (attain ends).

The 2-year-old is cognitively different from the infant at

birth. The infant is born with a few sensori-motor schemata (sucking, grasping, crying). The same child, two years later, bears little resemblance intellectually to the infant. At 2 he has a comparatively much larger and more sophisticated array of schemata. The evolution that occurs is primarily a function of the child's sensori-motor actions on the environment, resulting in ongoing assimilation and accommodation, that in turn results in qualitative and quantitative changes in schemata. Piaget (1968) writes:

> The period that extends from birth to the acquisition of language is marked by an extraordinary development of the mind. Its importance is sometimes underestimated because it is not accompanied by words that permit a step-by-step pursuit of the progress of intelligence and the emotions, as is the case later on. This early mental development nonetheless determines the entire course of psychological evolution. . . At the starting point of this development the neonate grasps everything to himself—or, in more precise terms, to his own body—whereas at the termination of the period, i.e., when language and thought begin, he is for all practical purposes but one element or entity among others in a universe that he has gradually constructed himself, and which hereafter he will experience as external to himself [pp. 8-9] .

To understand that the development of language in the two-year-old is related to earlier sensori-motor development, the observer must carefully observe behavior during the first two years of life. The evolution that occurs is a remarkably smooth succession of stages, each stage incorporating the previous stage, each marking a new advance.

Piaget (1952, 1954, 1967) divides the sensori-motor period into six stages (see Table 1) in which progressively more complex patterns of intellectual behavior evolve.

The remainder of this chapter will present aspects of the

six stages of sensori-motor development. The general characteristics of each stage will be discussed. These will include the progressive development of the child's *object* concept and his concept of *causality*, two of the most important indicators of intellectual development during this period.

What has previously been said about periods of development applies equally well to the stages of development about to be discussed. As behaviors evolve that are representative of a more advanced stage, the behaviors of previous stages are not totally displaced. Old, less sophisticated behaviors will still occur. Regarding new stages, Piaget (1964) writes:

> The new stage would thus be defined by the fact that the child becomes capable of certain behavior patterns of which he was up to then incapable; it is not the fact that he renounces the behavior patterns of the preceding stages, even if they are contrary to the new ones or contradictory to them from the observer's point of view [p. 299].

STAGE 1 (0-1 MONTH)

Beginning at birth and throughout most of the first stage of sensori-motor development, the behavior of the infant is entirely reflexive. The basic reflexes that the infant is born with are: sucking, grasping, crying, and movement of arms, trunk, and head. When the infant is stimulated, his reflexes respond. Thus, when an object is put in the infant's mouth, he sucks on it, regardless of what it is. When an object contacts the palm of the infant's hand, he grasps it, regardless of what it is. There is no evidence that the infant, behaving so, can differentiate between objects. His reflex responses are more or less the same to all objects. A blanket is sucked on as vigorously as a milk-producing nip-

TABLE 1

Characteristics of Development During the Sensori-Motor Period

Stage	General	Object Concept	Space	Causality
1 Reflex 0-1 mo.	Reflex activity	No differen- tiation of self from other objects	Egocentric	Egocentric
2 First dif- ferentiations 1-4 mos.	Hand-mouth co- ordination; differentiation via sucking, grasping	No special be- havior re vanished ob- jects; no differ- entiation of movement of self and ex- ternal objects	Changes in perspective seen as changes in objects	No differ- entiation of move- ment of self and external objects
3 Reproduction, 4-8 mos.	Eye-hand co- ordination; re- production of interesting events	Anticipates positions of moving objects	Space exter- nalized; no spacial rela- tionships of objects	Self seen as cause of all events

4 Coordination of schemata, 8-12 mos.	Coordination of schemata; application of known means to new problems; anticipation	Object permanence; searches for vanished objects; reverses bottle to get nipple	Perceptual constancy of size and shape of objects	Elementary externalization of causality
5 Experimentation, 12-18 mos.	Discovery of new means through experimentation	Considers sequential displacements while searching for vanished objects	Aware of relationships between objects in space, between objects and self	Self seen as object among objects and self as object of actions
6 Representation, 18-24 mos.	Representation; invention of new means via internal combinations	Images of absent objects, representation of displacements	Aware of movements not perceived; representation of spatial relationships	Representative causality; causes and effects inferred

ple. The hand grasps what comes into it, be it someone's finger or a toy. No distinction is made between stimuli. Thus, during this stage, the infant *assimilates* all stimuli through the reflex systems. At birth, all stimulus events are incorporated (assimilated) into primitive reflexive *schemata* in an undifferentiated manner.

Within a few weeks of birth, simple *accommodations* on the part of the child are usually observable. At birth the infant sucks on what is placed in its mouth. A nipple is sucked on when presented. Soon the infant begins to "search" for the nipple if it cannot be found; in effect, accommodating to the environment. The "searching" by the infant is a behavior that was not present at birth and cannot be attributed to any reflex system. There is no "searching" reflex; there is only a sucking reflex. Thus the active searching can be viewed as a change in reflex behavior on the part of the infant—an *accommodation*.

The innate, random reflex acts observable during the first stage undergo modification as a result of their repetitive use and interaction with the environment. While the young infant seems to be only exercising his reflexes when behaving, and no intellectual behaviors are observable, the *use* of the reflexes is essential for development during the stage and for the development of cognitive structures that are to follow. From the beginning, acts of assimilation and accommodation are present.

Object Concept

One of Piaget's important beliefs is that the object concept is not innate. That is, the awareness that objects are more or less permanent, and are not destroyed when they disappear, is not an inherited characteristic. He believes this awareness of objects is developed out of sensori-motor experiences little by little (Piaget, 1954, p. 4). In effect the child must reconstruct the universe of objects through his experiences. At birth, the infant has no awareness of objects. Indeed, the infant is unable to differentiate between himself and the environment. The infant has no concept of objects. Any object presented by the external environment is merely something to suck, to grasp, or to look at—something that evokes an undifferentiated reflexive response.

Concept of Causality

Causality, an awareness of cause and effect relationships, is another important concept that develops during the sensori-motor period. At birth the child is totally egocentric[1] and not aware of causality at all. It is not until later that awareness of causality begins to evolve.

STAGE 2 (1-4 MONTHS)

The second stage of sensori-motor development begins when the reflexive behaviors of the previous stage begin to be modified. During this stage several new behaviors appear. Thumb-sucking becomes habitual and reflects the development of hand-mouth coordination; moving objects are followed with the eyes (eye coordination); and the head is moved in the direction of sounds (eye-ear coordination).

---

[1] Egocentrism is one of Piaget's most important concepts. In general it refers to the cognitive state in which the individual sees the world only from his point of view, without being aware that other points of view exist. Thus it is a state that the egocentric cannot be aware of. For the infant, egocentrism means there is an absence of self-perception, of the self being an object in a world of objects. This is only overcome when the infant's concept of object develops and subsequently permits the development of self-perception.

Early in Stage 1, the infant's responses to stimuli are purely reflexive. No differentiation is initially made between stimuli. Toward the end of Stage 1 the infant distinguishes between objects, a behavior he could not perform at birth. For example, the infant actively sucks on a milk-producing nipple (when hungry), but rejects other objects that are placed in its mouth if it wants milk. A reflex has been modified, indicating that the infant has made an *accommodation* to the environment. Where a primitive sucking *schema* that did not permit differentiation had existed, a more sophisticated schema permitting differentiation now exists. Changes in behavior of this type are the first observable, if primitive, signs of the internal organization of and adaptation to the environment.

Habitual thumb-sucking is a behavior typically acquired during this stage (Piaget, *The Origins of Intelligence in Children*, 1952, p. 48). This new behavior requires hand-mouth coordination, an ability that the infant does not have during the first month. Prior to this time, thumb-sucking that occurs is usually a random or chance occurrence; the thumb happens to get into the mouth. Habituation of the activity cannot be explained by reflexes alone. It can only be explained by the child's discovery of sensori-motor relationships while acting on the environment.

Piaget (*The Origins of Intelligence in Children*, 1952, p. 53) illustrates the transition from random to clearly coordinated thumb-sucking:

> Observation 19.–At 0;1 (4)[2] after the 6 P.M. meal Laurent is wide awake (as was not the case at the preceding meals) and not completely satisfied. First he makes vigorous sucking-like

---

[2] 0;1 (4): Designations of this type make reference to the age of the child at the time of the observation, with years, months, days being referred to in that order. Laurent was 1 month, 4 days old at the time of observation.

movements, then his right hand may be seen approaching his mouth, touching his lower lip and finally being grasped. But as only the index finger was grasped, the hand fell out again. Shortly afterward it returned. This time the thumb was in the mouth while the index finger was placed between the gums and the upper lip. The hand then moves 5 cm. away from the mouth only to reenter it; now the thumb is grasped and the other fingers remain outside. Laurent then is motionless and sucks vigorously, drooling so much that after a few moments he is removed. A fourth time the hand approaches and three fingers enter the mouth. The hand leaves again and reenters a fifth time. As the thumb has again been grasped, sucking is resumed. I then remove the hand and place it near his waist. Laurent seems to give up sucking and gazes ahead, contented and satisfied. But after a few minutes the lips move and the hand approaches them again. This time there is a series of setbacks; the fingers are placed on the chin and lower lip. The index finger enters the mouth twice (consequently the sixth and seventh time this has succeeded). The eighth time the hand enters the mouth, the thumb alone is retained and sucking continues. I again remove the hand. Again lip movements cease, new attempts ensue, success results for the ninth and tenth time, after which the experiment is interrupted.

Laurent's thumb-sucking is rapidly becoming habitual. The behavior, since it is directed by the child, is different from all reflex behavior at birth. Such coordination implies an *accommodation* on the part of the child.

On the matter of thumb-sucking, Piaget (Ibid., p. 48) writes:

> When the child systematically sucks his thumb, no longer due to chance contacts but through coordination between hand and mouth, this may be called acquired accommodation. Neither the reflexes of the mouth nor of the hand can be provided such coordination by heredity (there is no instinct to suck the thumb!) and experience alone explains its formation.

During the second stage coordinations develop in the use of his eyes. The child begins to follow moving objects with the eyes. Piaget provides an example (Ibid., p. 63):

> Observation 28.—Jacqueline at 0;0(16) does not follow with her eyes the flame of a match 20 cm. away. Only her expression changes at the sight of it and then she moves her head as though to find the light again. She does not succeed despite the dim light in the room. At 0;0(24), on the other hand, she follows the match perfectly under the same conditions. The subsequent days her eyes follow the movements of my hand, a moving handkerchief, etc. From this date she can remain awake without crying, gazing ahead.

The ability to visually follow moving objects is not present at birth. As can be seen in Jacqueline's case, this ability is acquired.

Coordination between hearing and vision also develops at this time. Discriminations between sounds begin to occur. This is evident when children begin to move their heads in the direction of sounds, and when faces of people are clearly associated with sounds of the same person.

> Observation 48.—From 0;1(26) on the other hand, Laurent turns in the right direction as soon as he hears my voice (even if he has not seen me just before) and seems satisfied when he has discovered my face even when it is immobile. At 0;1(27) he looks successively at his father, his mother, and again at his father after hearing my voice. It therefore seems that he ascribes this voice to a visually familiar face. At 0;2(14) he observes Jacqueline at 1.90 to 2 meters, at the sound of her voice; same observation at 0;2(21). At 0;3(1) I squat before him while he is in his mother's arms and I make the sound bzz (which he likes). He looks to his left, then to his right, then ahead, then below him; then he catches sight of my hair and lowers his eyes until he sees my motionless face. Finally he smiles. This last observation may be considered as definitely

indicating identification of the voice and visual image of the person (Ibid., pp. 82-83).

These examples illustrate some of the cognitive differences between a typical child during the first month of life (Stage 1) and the next few months (Stage 2). The younger child makes undifferentiated reflex responses to stimuli. The older child makes primitive sensori-motor differentiations and acquires limited sensori-motor coordinations. These developments come about as the infant acts using his reflexes. Assimilation and accommodation produce initial changes in schemata.

Object Concept

During the second period of sensori-motor development the child evokes an awareness of objects that was not present during the first period. As was said earlier, the child tries to look at the objects he hears, indicating a coordination between vision and hearing. In addition, the child may continue to follow the path of an object with his eyes after it has disappeared from view. The following example from Piaget (1954) illustrates acquired visual following:

> Thus, Lucienne, at 0;3(9) sees me at the extreme left of her visual field and smiles vaguely. She then looks in different directions, in front of her and to the right, but constantly returns to the place in which she sees me and dwells on it every time for a moment [p. 10].

> At 0;4(26) she takes the breast but turns when I call her and smiles at me. Then she resumes nursing but several times in succession, despite my silence, she turns directly to the position from which she can see me. She does it again after a pause of a few minutes. Then I withdraw; when she turns without finding me her expression is one of mingled disappointment and expectation [pp. 10-11].

Lucienne (one of Piaget's daughters) demonstrates clearly she has coordination between hearing and vision. She locates visually the source of sounds. In addition, she is able to return and visually locate objects that have left her field of vision.

Intentionality

A number of new sensori-motor coordinations develop in Stage 2. The range of responses the infant makes increases. While advances have been made, the child's behavior still lacks *intention* in the sense that he initiates behaviors directed at certain ends. Behaviors are still primarily reflexive (though modified) and goals are set off only *after* behavior sequences are begun. Piaget writes (*The Origins of Intelligence in Children*, 1952, p.143):

> As long as action is entirely determined by directly perceived sensorial images, there can be no question of intention. Even when the child grasps an object in order to look at it, one cannot infer that there is a conscious purpose. It is with the appearance of... deferred reactions that the purpose of the action, ceasing to be in some way directly perceived, presupposes a continuity in searching, and consequently a beginning of intention.

Intentionality of behavior can only be inferred when the initiation of behaviors is not a reflex act or a simple repetition of preceding behavior.

Thus, the initial steps in intellectual development have begun. The child's actions in the environment, resulting in assimilations and accommodation, have produced primitive structural changes permitting simple sensori-motor coordinations. In the next stage these advances will be elaborated and surpassed through the same processes.

STAGE 3 (4-8 MONTHS)

During Stage 3, the child's behaviors become increasingly oriented toward objects and events beyond his body. The child grasps and manipulates all objects he can reach, signifying coordination between vision and tactile senses. Prior to this time, the infant's behavior has been oriented primarily toward himself. He has been unable to effectively distinguish himself from other objects on a sensorimotor level. He has been unable to coordinate the movement of his hands with his eyes.

Another characteristic of the third stage is that infants reproduce events that occur that are unusual to them. When interesting experiences occur, they try to repeat them. A cord attached to overhead bells is pulled repeatedly. Grasping and striking acts are repeated intentionally. There are clear attempts to sustain and repeat acts. Piaget (Ibid.) refers to this phenomenon as *reproductive assimilation*: the infant tries to reproduce events that are unique to him. As an illustration, Piaget (Ibid.) writes:

Observation 104.—At 0;3(29)Laurent grasps a paper knife which he sees for the first time; he looks at it a moment and then swings it while holding it in his right hand. During these movements the object happens to rub against the wicker of the bassinet: Laurent then waves his arms vigorously and obviously tries to reproduce the sound he has heard, but without understanding the necessity of contact between the paper knife and the wicker and, consequently, without achieving this contact otherwise than by chance.

At 0;4(3) same reactions, but Laurent looks at the object at the time when it happens to rub against the wicker of the bassinet. The same still occurs at 0;4(5) but there is slight progress towards systematization.

> Finally, at 0;4(6) the movement becomes intentional; as
> soon as the child has the object in his hand he rubs it with
> regularity against the wicker of the bassinet. . .[pp. 168-169].

When a child successfully repeats previous behaviors, as
Laurent did in the example, primitive sensori-motor intentionality is evident.

Intentionality

One of the characteristics of the sensori-motor period is
the child's progress from non-intentional behavior to a
type of intentional behavior. During the second period of
sensori-motor development, intentional behavior is not evident. At that time behavior is random and elicited by
stimulation. It is not designed to attain a goal or object.
During Stage 3, the child begins to engage in a type of
goal-directed (intentional) behavior. He tries to repeat unusual and interesting events. In Stage 3, goals are established only *after* behaviors have begun. The infant's goals
become established only during the repetitions of behaviors, and consequently, the intentionality (goal direction)
is after the fact, so to speak, after behavior has begun. In
later stages (Stage 4), the infant *initiates* a behavior sequence with a goal to be attained, and selects means that
will attain the goal. Intentionality is present at the beginning of the sequence, and thus the behavior is not a mere
repetition of a previous behavior, but an intentional act.
Thus while behavior in Stage 3 is for the first time intentional, it is not intentional until after behavior sequences
have begun.

Object Concept

During period 3 the child begins to anticipate positions
objects will pass through while they are moving. This indi-

cates that the child's awareness of the permanence of objects is developing. The following example from Piaget (1954) illustrates this:

> Observation 6.—Laurent's reaction to falling objects still seems to be nonexistent at 0;5(24): he does not follow with his eyes any of the objects which I drop in front of him . . .
>
> At 0;5(30) no reaction to the fall of a box of matches. The same is true at 0;6(0), but when he drops the box himself he searches for it next to him with his eyes (he is lying down) . . .
>
> At 0;6(7) he holds an empty match box in his hand. When it falls his eyes search for it even if they have not followed the beginning of the fall; he turns his head in order to see it on the sheet. Same reaction at 0;6(9) with a rattle . . .
>
> At 0;7(29) he searches on the floor for everything I drop above him, if he has in the least perceived the beginning of the movement of falling . . . [pp. 14-15] .

In the example, Laurent by 8 months of age is looking for objects in places where he predicts they have fallen. He is anticipating positions falling objects will assume, demonstrating a more sophisticated schema of object than in previous stages.

Concept of Causality

During Stage 3 the child remains egocentric. He sees himself as the primary cause of all activity. The following example illustrates the child's egocentric awareness of causality during Stage 3. Piaget (1954) writes:

> At 0;7(8) Laurent is seated and I place a large cushion within his reach. I scratch the cushion. He laughs. Afterward I move my hand five cm. from the cushion, between it and his own hands, in such a way that if he pushed it slightly it would press against the cushion. As soon as I pause, Laurent strikes the cushion, arches, swings his head, etc. True, subsequently he

does sometimes grasp my hand. But it is only in order to strike it, shake it, etc., and he does not once try to move it forward or put it in contact with the cushion.

At a certain moment he scratches my hand; on the other hand, he does not scratch the cushion although this behavior is familiar to him [p. 245].

Clearly, Laurent believes he alone can cause events. He is not aware that his father's hand is causing the interesting sound when it is in contact with the cushion. He shakes his father's hand to make the sound; he scratches the hand. He acts on the hand and on the cushion, but never on the two together. To the child, he himself is the cause of all events.

STAGE 4 (8-12 MONTHS)

Toward the end of the first year of life, behavior patterns emerge that constitute the first clear acts of intelligence. The infant begins to use means to attain ends; he begins to anticipate events, demonstrating prevision. Objects take on a noticeable measure of permanence for the child. He begins to search for objects that he sees disappear. Also, he comes to see that other objects in the environment can be sources of activity (causality).

Prior to this stage, behavior has always been a direct action of the child on objects. Interesting acts are prolonged or repeated. That is, a single *schema* had been used to evoke a behavioral response. During Stage 4 the child begins to coordinate two familiar schemata in generating a single act: he begins to use means to attain ends that are not immediately attainable in a direct way. Children can be seen to set aside one object (means) to get to another object (end). A pillow is moved out of the way to reach a toy. There is an *intentional* selection of means prior to the initiation of behavior. The end is established from the beginning, the means being used precisely in order to reach the end. The following example from Piaget (*The Origins of Intelligence in Children*, 1952) illustrates the means-ends coordination that develops:

> Observation 121.—At 0;8(20) Jacqueline tries to grasp a ciga-rette case which I present to her. I then slide it between the crossed strings which attach her dolls to the hood (of her bassinet). She tries to reach it directly. Not succeeding, she immediately looks for the strings which are not in her hands and of which she only saw the part in which the cigarette case is entangled. She looks in front of her, grasps the strings, pulls and shakes them, etc. The cigarette case then falls and she grasps it.
>
> Second experiment: same reaction, but without first trying to grasp the object directly [p. 215].

In the example Jacqueline pulls the strings (means) to attain the cigarette case (end). Clearly this is an intentional act from the outset. Means and ends (two schemata) are coordinated in one action.

During Stage 4, the infant shows clear signs of anticipation of events. Certain "signs" are recognized as being associated with certain actions that follow the signs. These actions illustrate prevision and the "meaning" of certain events.

> Observation 132.—At 0;8(6) Laurent recognizes by a certain noise caused by air that he is nearing the end of his feeding and, instead of insisting on drinking to the last drop, he rejects his bottle . . .
>
> Observation 133.—At 0;9(15) Jacqueline wails or cries when she sees the person seated next to her get up or move away a little (giving the impression of leaving) . . .
>
> At 1;1(10) she has a slight scratch which is disinfected with alcohol. She cries, chiefly from fear. Subsequently, as soon as she again sees the bottle of alcohol she recommences to cry,

knowing what is in store for her. Two days later, same reaction, as soon as she sees the bottle and even before it is opened [Ibid., pp. 248-249] .

Such behavior clearly demonstrates anticipation or prevision on the part of the child. An action is anticipated that is independent of the action in progress. During preceding stages actions of the child were *always* dependent on the immediate actions in the environment. Jacqueline would cry when alcohol was put on a cut, not before it was put on.

Object Concept

The most important acquisition of this stage is undoubtedly that of the constancies of shape and size of objects. Commenting on shape and size constancy, Piaget and Inhelder (1956) write:

In fact, the *constancy of shapes* results from their sensorimotor construction at the time of the coordination of perspectives. During the first period (0-4 mos.) . . . when objects change their perspective such alterations are perceived (by the child) not as changes in the point of view of the subject relative to the object, but as actual transformations of the objects themselves. The baby waggling his head before a hanging object behaves as if he acted upon it by jerking about, and it is not until the age of about 8-9 months that he really explores the perspective effects of actual displacements. Now it is just about this age (8-9 mos.) that he is first able . . . to reverse a feeding bottle presented to him wrong way round. That is, to attribute a fixed shape to a permanent solid.

As for *size constancy* it is linked with the coordination of perceptually controlled movements. All through the first period (0-4 mos.) the child makes no distinction between movements of the object and those of his body . . . In the course of the second period (Stage 3 and 4) the subject begins to distinguish his own movements from those of the object. Here is found the beginning . . . of searching for objects when they disappear. It is in terms of this grouping of movements, and the permanence attributed to the object, that the latter acquires fixed dimensions and its size is estimated more or less correctly, regardless of whether it is near or distant [p. 11].

As with other concepts, those of size and constancy develop in the expected manner. Different perspectives on objects appear to the 4-month-old child to change the shape and size of the objects. Not until Stage 4 are shape and size of objects stabilized concepts for the child.

During period 4 a new dimension in the object concept of the child appears. Up until this time, if an object such as a rattle is placed under a blanket while the child is looking on, the child does not search after it. If an object is out of sight, it no longer exists to the child. Between the ages of 8 and 10 months (approximately) the child begins to search for objects that disappear. The rattle hidden under the blanket is retrieved. The following illustration from Piaget (1954) illustrates this new awareness of object permanence and some of its limitations:

Observation 40 —At 0;10(18) Jacqueline is seated on a mattress without anything to disturb or distract her (no coverlets, etc.). I take her parrot from her hands and hide it twice in succession under the mattress, on her left, in A. Both times Jacqueline looks for the object immediately and grabs it. Then I take it from her hands and move it very slowly before her eyes to the corresponding place on her right, under the mattress, in B (sequential displacement). Jacqueline watches this movement very attentively, but at the moment when the parrot disappears in B, she turns to her left and looks where it was before, in A.

During the next four attempts I hide the parrot in B every time without having first placed it in A. Each time Jacqueline watches me attentively. Nevertheless each time she immediately tries to rediscover the object in A; she turns the mattress over and examines it conscientiously . . . [p. 51] .

Clearly, Jacqueline searches for objects that disappear. To do this she must have a concept that objects still exist after they disappear from view. But her searches are limited; she only searches for objects where they usually disappear, not always where they are viewed to disappear.

Concept of Causality

During Stage 4 the child for the first time shows awareness that objects (besides himself) can cause activity. Up until this time, the child typically considers his own actions as the source of all causality. This change in the concept of causality is illustrated by Piaget (1954):

> 0;8(7) . . . (Laurent) . . . A moment later I lower my hand very slowly, starting very high up and directing it toward his feet, finally tickling him for a moment. He bursts out laughing. When I stop midway, he grasps my hand or arm and pushes it toward his feet . . .
> . . . At 0;9(0) he grasps my hand and places it against his belly which I have just tickled . . .
> . . . At 0;9(13) Laurent is in his baby swing which I shake three or four times by pulling a cord; he grasps my hand and presses it against the cord [p. 261] .

Piaget (*The Origins of Intelligence in Children*, 1952) comments:

> . . . the cause of a certain phenomenon is no longer identified by the child with the feeling he has of acting upon this phenomenon. The subject begins to discover that a spatial contact exists between cause and effect and so any object at all can be a source of activity (and not only his own body) [p. 212] .

For the first time, there is an elementary externalization of causality. The child is aware that objects can be the causes of actions.

STAGE 5 (12-18 MONTHS)

In the previous stages the child developed coordination between schemata for vision and touch permitting him to prolong unusual events (Stage 3), subsequently becoming able to coordinate familiar schemata in solving *new* problems (Stage 4). In Stage 5 the child attains a higher level of operation when he begins to form *new* schemata to solve new problems. The child develops *new* means to ends through "experimentation" rather than through the application of habitual, previously formed schemata. In this case both *new* schemata and *new* coordinations are present. When confronted with a problem not solvable by the use of available schemata, the child can be seen to experiment and, through a trial-and-error process, develop *new* means (schemata). This can be seen in several examples from Piaget (Ibid.):

> Observation 167.—At 1;3(12) Jacqueline throws a plush dog outside the bars of her playpen and she tries to catch it. Not succeeding, she then pushes the pen itself in the right direction! By holding onto the frame with one hand while with the other she tried to grasp the dog, she observed that the frame was mobile. She had accordingly, without wishing to do so, moved it away from the dog. She at once tried to correct this movement and thus saw the pen approach its objective. These two fortuitous discoveries then led her to utilize movements of the playpen and to push it at first experimentally, then systematically. There was a moment's groping, but it was short.
>
> At 1;3(16), on the other hand, Jacqueline right away pushes her playpen in the direction of the objects to be picked up [p. 315].

In the example, Jacqueline "experiments" with playpen moving. The utility of this behavior evolves after much trial-and-error experimentation. With experience a *new* schema is developed (playpen moving) that results in the solution of a problem previously unsolvable to the child.

In the first half of the second year, the child spends much time "experimenting" with objects as in the example above. In the bathtub, objects are repeatedly pushed under water; things are splashed. The child typically is very intent on seeing how objects behave in *new* situations. For the first time, the child truly adapts (accommodates) himself to unfamiliar situations by finding new means. Prior to Stage 5 behavior was primarily assimilatory in nature.

In terms of intellectual development, these new behaviors are particularly important. Piaget (Ibid.) suggests that behavior becomes intelligent when the child acquires the ability to solve new problems.

> . . . it can be said that the mechanism of empirical intelligence has been definitely formed. The child is henceforth capable of resolving new problems, even if no acquired (currently available) schema is directly utilizable for this purpose, and if the solution of these problems has not yet been found by deduction or representation, it is insured in principle in all cases due to the combined working of experimental search and the coordination of schemata [p. 265].

The child has reached a significant period in cognitive development when he becomes able to solve new sensorimotor problems. It marks the beginning of truly intelligent behavior in the child, the development of which started when reflex activities began in the young infant.

Object Concept

Around the age of 12 months the child's behavior indicates an awareness that objects continue to exist even though they cannot be seen. Prior to Stage 4 the child did not search for objects that were hidden, even though he viewed the disappearance. The rattle hidden under the blanket was not retrieved. In Stage 4 (8-12 months) the child searches for objects that are hidden, but not always in the place where they are seen to be hidden. In this case the child was said to be unable to handle *sequential displacements*, i.e., if the rattle which is usually hidden in place A now is hidden in place B, the child searched for it in place A. In Stage 5 the child learns to account for sequential displacements; he searches for objects in the position resulting from the last visible displacement, not in a special place. When the rattle is hidden in A, it is searched for in A; when it is hidden in B, it is searched for in B.

Still the object concept is not yet fully developed. The child during Stage 5 typically is able to follow displacements if they are visible, but he remains unable to follow *invisible displacements*. The following interesting example illustrates this case:

Observation 56.— . . . at 1;6(9), I resume the experiment but with a celluloid fish containing a rattle. I put the fish in the box and the box under the rug. There I shake it and Jacqueline hears the fish in the box. I turn the box upside down and bring it out empty. Jacqueline immediately takes possesion of the box, searches for the fish, turns the box over in all directions, looks around her, in particular looks at the rug but does not raise it.

The next attempts yield nothing further . . .

That evening I repeat the experiment with a little lamb.

> Jacqueline herself puts the lamb in the box and when the whole thing is under the coverlet she says with me, "Coucou, lamb." When I take out the empty box she says, "Lamb, Lamb," but does not look under the coverlet.
>
> Whenever I leave the whole thing under the coverlet she immediately searches for the box and brings out the lamb. But when I start again, using the first technique, she no longer looks under the coverlet! [Piaget, 1954, p.69].

While the abilities developed during Stage 5 permit Jacqueline to solve problems involving sequential displacements, she cannot yet solve those involving invisible displacements. This ability will not come about until she develops mental representation of objects (Stage 6).

Concept of Causality

In the previous stage the typical child demonstrates an awareness that other objects beyond himself can be a source of actions (causality). The following example illustrates the elaboration of the concept of causality in Stage 5:

> At 1;3(30) Jacqueline holds in her right hand a box she cannot open. She holds it out to her mother, who pretends not to notice. Then she transfers the box from her right hand to her left, with her free hand grasps her mother's hand, opens it, and puts the box in it. The whole thing has occurred without a sound . . .
>
> So also, during the next days, Jacqueline makes the adult intervene in the particulars of her game, whenever an object is too remote, etc.: she calls, cries, points to objects with her fingers, etc. In short, she well knows that she depends on the adult for satisfaction; the person of someone else becomes her best procedure for realization [Ibid., p. 275].

Not only does Jacqueline demonstrate an awareness that other people can effect activity, but also that other objects can. The following illustration shows this clearly:

Observation 175.—At 1;2(30) Jacqueline is standing in a room which is not hers and examines the green wallpaper. Then she touches it gently and at once looks at her fingertips. This is evidently the generalization of schemata . . . touching food (jams, etc.) and looking at her fingers . . .

At 1;3(12) she is standing in her playpen and I place a clown, which she recently received, on the top of the frame, in different places in sequence. Jacqueline advances laboriously along the frame but, when she arrives in front of the clown, she grasps it very cautiously and delicately, knowing that it will fall at the slightest shake. She behaved in this way ever since the first attempt. . . . Jacqueline foresees certain properties of the object which are independent of its action with respect to herself. The green wallpaper is conceived as though it ought to leave colored traces, . . . and the clown as falling down at the first touch [Piaget, *The Origins of Intelligence in Children*, 1952, pp. 327-328] .

In these examples Jacqueline clearly sees objects (wallpaper, clown) as the causes of possible phenomena that are external to her actions. Prevision is seen that is *not* based on sequences of actions already observed in the same form (the wallpaper and doll are new to Jacqueline). Thus objects beyond the self are for the first time seen as causes of actions.

STAGE 6 (18-24 MONTHS)

During Stage 6 the child moves from the sensori-motor level of intelligence to representational intelligence. That is, the child becomes able to internally (mentally) represent objects and subsequently becomes able to solve problems through representation (cognitively). In Stage 5, new means for solutions to problems were attained through active experimentation. In Stage 6 the child develops new means also, but there is no appearance of experimentation as in the previous stage. Invention of means is arrived at suddenly. The following example illustrates Stage 6 invention of means, through representation and mental activity:

> Observation 181.—At 1;6(23) for the first time Lucienne plays with a doll carriage whose handle comes to the height of her face. She rolls it over the carpet by pushing it. When she comes against a wall, she pulls, walking backward. But as this position is not convenient for her, she pauses and without hesitation, goes to the other side to push the carriage again. She therefore found the procedure in one attempt, apparently through analogy to other situations but without training, apprenticeship, or chance.
>
> In the same kind of inventions, that is to say, in the realm of kinematic[3] representations, the following fact should be cited. At 1;10(27) Lucienne tries to kneel before a stool, but, by leaning against it, pushes it further away. She then raises herself up, takes it and places it against a sofa. When it is firmly set there she leans against it and kneels without difficulty [Ibid., p. 338].

Lucienne, in these examples, demonstrates the sudden invention of a solution to sensori-motor problems along with an awareness of causality. The suddenness of the inventions and the lack of experimentation suggest that solutions are arrived at internally through mental combinations, independent of immediate experiences. Piaget explains:

> . . . instead of being controlled at each of these stages and *a posteriori* by the facts themselves, the searching is controlled *a priori* by mental combination. Before trying them, the child foresees which maneuvers will fail and which will succeed . . . Moreover, the procedure conceived as being capable of succeeding is in itself new, that is to say, it results from an origi-

---

[3] The science of motions considered apart from their causes and as applied to mechanical contrivances.

nal mental combination and not from a combination of movements actually executed at each stage of the operation [Ibid., pp. 340-341].

Thus the child becomes able to solve problems internally. For about two years this ability has been gradually evolving from sensori-motor behaviors. At this stage the child can arrive at solutions to simple motor problems without the aid of experimentation or the assistance of concurrent experiences.

Object Concept

The ability of the Stage 6 child to internally represent events is reflected in the child's object concept. Representation allows the child to find objects that are hidden by invisible displacement. That is, the child cannot only find objects where they are visibly hidden, but representation permits the child to search for, and find, objects that he does not see hidden. This amounts to a liberation from immediate perceptions. The child knows objects are permanent. The following observation of Jacqueline demonstrates this awareness:

Observation 64.—At 1;7(20) Jacqueline watches me when I put a coin in my hand, then put my hand under a coverlet. I withdraw my hand closed; Jacqueline opens it, then searches under the coverlet until she finds the object. I take back the coin at once, put it in my hand and then slip my closed hand under a cushion situated at the other side (on her left and no longer on her right); Jacqueline immediately searches for the object under the cushion. I repeat the experiment by hiding the coin under a jacket; Jacqueline finds it without hesitation.

II. I complicate the test as follows: I place the coin in my hand, then my hand under the cushion. I bring it forth closed and immediately hide it under the coverlet. Finally I withdraw it and hold it out, closed, to Jacqueline. Jacqueline then pushes my hand aside without opening it (she guesses that there is nothing in it, which is new), she looks under the cushion, then directly under the coverlet where she finds the object . . .

I then try a series of three displacements: I put the coin in my hand and move my closed hand sequentially from A to B and from B to C; Jacqueline sets my hand aside, then searches in A, in B and finally in C.

Lucienne is successful in the same tests at 1;3(14) [Piaget 1954, p. 79].

The ability of the child to maintain "images" of objects when they are absent is clearly seen in the above example. The displacement of objects results in a search on the part of the child until they are found.

Concept of Causality

As with the object concept and other development, the child's awareness of causality is greatly enhanced by his new ability to internally represent objects. Through Stage 5 the child remains unable to predict true cause-effect relationships in his sensori-motor world. Piaget writes (1954):

Just as during the sensorimotor development of objects and the spatial field the child becomes capable of evoking absent objects and of representing to himself displacements not given as such in the perceptual field, so also at the sixth stage the child becomes capable of reconstructing causes in the presence of their effects alone, and without having perceived the action of those causes. Inversely, given a certain perceived object as the source of potential actions, he becomes capable of foreseeing and representing to himself its future effects [p. 293].

The following example demonstrates Laurent's concept of causality at this stage. Clearly through representation he accurately predicts a cause and effect relationship.

At 1;4(4) . . . Laurent tries to open a garden gate but cannot push it forward because it is held back by a piece of furniture. He cannot account either visually or by any sound for the cause that prevents the gate from opening, but after having tried to force it he suddenly seems to understand; he goes around the wall, arrives at the other side of the gate, moves the armchair which holds it firm, and opens it with a triumphant expression [Ibid., p. 296].

Again, the rapid invention of solution to problems is seen. Such solutions were not seen in behaviors prior to Stage 6. Laurent demonstrates representation of objects, a clear object concept, and a clear understanding of causality in a sensori-motor problem. Piaget (Ibid.) writes:

In a general way, therefore, at the sixth stage the child is now capable of causal deduction and is no longer restricted to perception or sensorimotor utilization of the relations of cause to effect [p. 297].

SUMMARY OF THE
SENSORI-MOTOR PERIOD OF DEVELOPMENT

The child at age 2 is cognitively different from the infant at birth. This chapter has presented Piaget's conceptualization of how this transformation takes place. The child at birth performs only reflex activity. Toward the second month of life, the infant makes primitive differentiations of objects in its immediate environment, primarily via the sucking reflex. Between the fourth and eighth months, co-ordination of vision and touch typically occurs for the first time. The child grasps what it sees (Stage 3). Toward the end of the first year the child begins to develop object permanence and an awareness that objects besides himself can cause events. Two familiar schemata are coordinated to solve new problems (Stage 4). Early in the second year, true intelligent behavior typically occurs; the child evolves *new* means to solving problems through "experimentation." Also he sees himself as an object among objects (Stage 5). Toward the end of the second year, the child becomes able to internally represent objects. This ability liberates him from sensori-motor intelligence, permitting the invention of *new* means to solve problems through mental activity.

The cognitive development of the sensori-motor period evolves as the child *acts* on the environment. The adapting and organizing of assimilation and accommodation operate from the beginning, resulting in the continuous qualitative and quantitative change in schemata. Each new stage is characterized by behaviors reflecting qualitatively superior cognitive structures. Thus in the development of intelligence during the first two years of life, it can be seen that each new stage of development incorporates previous stages. The new stages do not displace the old, they merely improve upon them. In the same way, each stage of development helps to explain stages that follow. So it is throughout the course of cognitive development.

As the infant develops cognitively, there is a concurrent and related development of *all* concepts. Concepts do not develop independent of one another. For example, in Stage 4 (8-12 months), the typical child for the first time becomes able to systematically turn a bottle around so he can get the nipple. What does this imply about the child's concepts or schemata? First of all, the behavior suggests the child is aware of the constancy of shape of objects. Objects do not change in shape when perspectives on them change (object concept). Since all actions occur in space, the child must also have a functional concept of space and the relationships between objects. Also, the behavior of turning the bottle around is clearly an *intentional* act requiring a measure of hand-eye *coordination*. Each of these abilities evolves at about the same time. Their paths of development are one. As the child assimilates and accommodates, all his schemata are elaborated. Thus it is that evolving behaviors reflect qualitative changes in many schemata.

Upon completing the development of the sensori-motor period (it can be before or after age 2), the child has reached a point of conceptual development that is necessary for the development of language and other cognitive skills during the next major period in cognitive development: the preoperational period. From this point on, the child's intellectual development will take place primarily in the conceptual-symbolic area rather than in the sensori-motor area. This does not imply that sensori-motor development ends, only that intellectual development is to be dominated by representational and symbolic activity rather than by motor activity.

Chapter Four

II

The Period of
Preoperational Thought

During the preoperational period (ages 2 to 7 years) the child evolves from one who functions primarily in a sensori-motor mode to one who functions primarily in a conceptual-symbolic mode. The child becomes increasingly able to internally represent events (think) and becomes less dependent on his direct sensori-motor actions for direction of behavior.

Between the ages of 2 and 7 the child's thought is characterized by new emerging abilities. Several of the most important characteristics of preoperational thought will be discussed. The development of language and the socialization of behavior will be presented first. This will be followed by a discussion of characteristics of thought that, while necessary, prevent the preoperational child from attaining completely logical, or "adult-like" thought. These are egocentrism, centration, irreversibility, and inability to follow transformations.

LANGUAGE

The single most important development during the preoperational period is the development of language. Around 2 years of age (give or take a few months), the child begins to use words as symbols in place of objects. A word comes to represent an object. Initially the child uses "one-word" sentences, but his language facility expands quickly. By the age of 4 the typical child has mastered the use of language. He can speak and use most grammatical rules, and he can understand when he is spoken to. The rapid development of symbolic representation (language) is instrumental in facilitating the very rapid conceptual development that takes place during this period.

The acquisition of language profoundly affects intellectual life. Piaget (1968) writes:

> This [language] has three consequences essential to mental development: (1) the possibility of verbal exchange with other persons, which heralds the onset of the socialization of action; (2) the internalization of words, i.e., the appearance of thought itself, supported by internal language and a system of signs; (3) last and most important, the internalization of action of such which from now on, rather than being purely perceptual and motor as it has been heretofore, can represent itself intuitively by means of pictures and "mental experiments" [p. 17].

Language opens doors to the child that were not open before. The internalization of behavior through representation, facilitated by language, acts to "speed up" the rate at which experience can take place.

Piaget (1926) suggests, on the basis of his observations of young children's conversations, that there are essentially two different classifications of the preoperational child's speech: (1) egocentric speech, and (2) socialized speech. Egocentric speech is characterized by a lack of real communication. Socialized speech, on the other hand, is characterized by communication. From the ages of 2 to 4 or 5, the child's speech is largely lacking in communicative intent. He speaks in the presence of others, but without any apparent intention that others should hear his words. Even though the child speaks with others, there is no communication. Nonconversations of this type Piaget calls *collective monologues*. Speech of this type is clearly egocentric. The following example from Piaget (Ibid) demonstrates the non-communicative egocentric speech of the early preoperational child:

> Mlle. L. tells a group of children that owls cannot see by day.
> Lev: "Well, I know quite well that it can't."
> Lev (at a table where a group is at work): "I've already done moon so I'll have to change it."
> Lev picks up some barley sugar crumbs: "I say, I've got a lovely pile of eye-glasses."
> Lev: "I say, I've got a gun to kill him with. I say, I am the captain on horseback. I say, I've got a horse and a gun as well" [p. 41].

These examples of speech are clearly egocentric. Lev is simply thinking out his actions aloud, with no desire to give anyone any information. He is having a conversation with himself in the presence of others (collective monologue).

By the ages of 6 or 7 years, language has become intercommunicative. Children's conversations clearly involve an exchange of ideas. In the following example, Lev, now considerably older than in the previous example, communicates with others in his conversations:

> Pie (6;5): "Now, you shan't have it [the pencil] because you asked for it.—" Hei (6;0): "Yes I will, because it's mine.—" Pie: "Course it isn't yours. It belongs to everybody, to all the children." —Lev (6;0): "Yes, it belongs to Mlle. L. and all the children. . ." Pie: "It belongs to Mlle. L. because she bought it, and it belongs to all the children as well" [Ibid., p. 88].

Clearly, the above illustration involves communication. Lev in the earlier example spoke only to himself. In the last he spoke to others and clearly intended them to hear.

The development of language during the preoperational period is seen by Piaget as a gradual transition from egocentric speech characterized by *collective monologue* to socialized intercommunicative speech.

LANGUAGE AND THOUGHT

The relationship between language and thought is an important one. Piaget's formulation of sensori-motor development demonstrates that the rudiments of intelligent behavior evolve *before* language develops. Regarding the relationship between intelligence and language, Piaget (1967) writes:

> Intelligence actually appears well before language, that is to say, well before internal thought, which presupposes the use of verbal signs (internalized language). It is an entirely practical intelligence based on the manipulation of objects; in place of words and concepts it uses percepts and movements organized into "action schema." For example, to grab a stick in order to draw up a remote object is an act of intelligence (and a fairly late developing one at that: about eighteen months). Here, an instrument, the means to an end, is coordinated with a pre-established goal...Many other examples could be cited [p. 11].

Piaget contends that the emergence of verbal behavior increases the powers of thought in range and speed. He suggests that there are three major differences between verbal and sensori-motor behavior: (1) the sequence of events in sensori-motor patterns is restricted to the speed of sensori-motor acts, making sensori-motor intelligence very slow. On the other hand, verbal behavior permits the representation of many actions very quickly. (2) Sensori-motor adaptations are limited to the immediate actions of

the child, while language permits thought and adaptation
to range beyond present activity. (3) Sensori-motor intelligence proceeds in a one-step-at-a-time fashion, while representational thought and language permit the child to
simultaneously handle many elements in an organized
manner (Piaget and Inhelder, 1969, p. 86).

Thus, because language is a form of representation of
objects and events, thought involving language is liberated
from the limitations of the direct action of sensori-motor
thought. Cognitive activity can proceed rapidly and with a
range and speed not previously available.

Another important question is whether language (in a
simplistic sense) determines logical thought or whether
thought determines language. Every language has a logical
structure that is a socially elaborated system for relationships, classifications, and so on. The child does not "invent" language or the logic of language. Does this mean
that the logic of language is the source of all the logic of
the child, or does the child invent and create his own
logic? Piaget and Inhelder (Ibid) cite two types of studies
that support their contention that language is neither a
necessary nor sufficient condition to ensure the development of logical thought. Studies of deaf mutes (no verbal
language) show that they develop logical thought in the
same sequential stages as normal children, but with a 1 to
2 year delay in some operations (p. 88). This suggests that
language is not necessary for the development of logical
operations though it clearly acts as a facilitator. Other
studies of blind children, with normal verbal development,
demonstrate longer delays, up to four years on the same
tasks (p. 88). Blind children are hindered from birth in the
development of sensori-motor schemata, and normal verbal
performance does not compensate for this.

For Piaget the development of language is based on the prior development of sensori-motor operations. Thus, it is the development of sensori-motor operations that are necessary for language development, and not the other way around. When language develops there is a parallel development of conceptual abilities that language helps to facilitate, probably because language and representation permit conceptual activity to proceed more rapidly than sensori-motor operations do. The development of sensori-motor schemata is seen as a prerequisite to language development (as in blind children). Language development is seen as a facilitator of cognitive development (as in deaf children) but not as a prerequisite.

SOCIALIZATION OF BEHAVIOR

Behavior is considered social when it involves clear interchanges of ideas between people. The process of socialization begins long before behavior is social. Socialization can be traced back to the latter part of the first year of life when the child first begins to imitate other people. The process of imitation (a type of accommodation) develops until the child shows deferred imitation (imitation of absent objects) around age 2. During the preoperational period, socialization of the child's behavior can be seen in several types of activities including children's verbal exchanges and their play in games with rules (Piaget and Inhelder, 1969, p. 119).

The discussion of language pointed out that during the early part of the preoperational period, children's verbal interactions are primarily composed of collective monologue conversations. Children speak in the presence of others as if they are speaking to themselves. They do not ask questions or exchange information. Verbal behavior is not communicative and not truly social. Not until ages 6 to 7 does most of children's verbal behavior become clearly communicative and social.

Games with rules also reflect children's social development. In games with rules, such as marbles, the rules are passed on from generation to generation without alteration. The young child (4 to 5 years) does not understand rules and consequently plays marbles as he understands the game. He plays as if by himself. Everybody can win. There is no collective rule to guide behavior. Around the age of 7 or 8, children become concerned with winning and with rules. Cooperation appears in these games for the first time. There is a common awareness and observance of rules and all players make sure the rules are followed. These behaviors are clearly social (Piaget, 1932).

OBSTACLES TO THE DEVELOPMENT OF LOGICAL THOUGHT

Piaget suggests that there are three levels of relationship between the actions of the child and his thought. The first is the sensori-motor level of direct action upon the environment. Between birth and age 2 all schemata are sensori-motor and dependent on the actions of the child. And the third, after ages 7 or 8, is the level of operations or logical thought. The child becomes able to reason in a way that is not dependent on immediate perceptual and motor actions (period of concrete operations). Between the two, ages 2 to 7, is the preoperational period (the second level), which is an advance over sensori-motor intelligence, but is not as advanced as the logical operations of later periods. Cognitive behavior is still influenced by perceptual activities. Actions are internalized via symbolic functions, but thought is not liberated from perception. (Piaget and Inhelder, 1969, p. 93)

The characteristics of preoperational thought to be discussed are necessary for continuous development. In addition, they serve as obstacles to logical thought. The "obstacles" to logical thought that are presented are: egocentrism, transformations, centration, and reversibility.

Egocentrism

Piaget characterizes the preoperational child's behavior and thinking as *egocentric*. That is, the child cannot take the role of or see the viewpoint of another. He believes that everyone thinks the same way he does, and that everyone thinks the same things he does. As a result, the child never questions his own thoughts because they are, as far as he is concerned, the only thoughts possible and consequently must be correct.

The preoperational child does not reflect on his own thoughts. As a result, he is never motivated to question his thinking, even when he is confronted with evidence that is contradictory to his thoughts. In such cases, the egocentric child concludes the evidence must be wrong, because his thoughts cannot be. Thus, the child's thinking, from his point of view, is always quite logical and correct.

This egocentrism of thought is not egocentric by intent. The child remains unaware that he is egocentric and consequently never seeks to resolve it. Egocentrism is manifest in all the behavior of the preoperational child. As stated before, the 2- to 6-year-old's language and social behavior are largely egocentric. The child talks to himself when in the presence of others (in collective monologues) and does not listen to others. Verbal behavior involves very little exchange of information and is non-social for the most part.

It is not until around the ages of 6 or 7 when children's thoughts and those of their peers clearly conflict, that children begin to accommodate to others and egocentric thought begins to give way to social pressure. Peer group social interaction, the repeated conflict of one's own thoughts with those of others, eventually jars the child to question and seek verification of his thoughts. The very source of conflict, social interaction, becomes the child's source of verification. To be sure, verification of one's thoughts only comes about through comparison with the thoughts of others. Thus, peer group social interaction is the primary factor that acts to dissolve cognitive egocentrism.

While egocentrism pervades the behavior of the preoperational child, it should not be thought that egocentric behavior does not occur in other periods of development. The sensori-motor child is totally egocentric at birth (in a sensori-motor sense: unable to differentiate himself from other objects), and continues to be so throughout the first two years of life. Indeed, egocentrism is a characteristic of thought that is *always* present during the initial attainment and use of any new cognitive structure (schema). Later it will be seen that the adolescent, upon developing completely logical thought, is very egocentric in his use of the newly acquired structures. Like other cognitive characteristics, egocentrism is not at a constant level throughout the period. The child from 2 to 4 is much more consistently egocentric than the child from 6 to 7. As development proceeds, egocentrism slowly wanes until it is revived when new cognitive structures are attained. Thus, egocentrism is a characteristic that pervades thought in some way in all periods of development.

Egocentric thinking, while a necessary characteristic of preoperational thought, in a sense acts to restrict the development of intellectual structures during the preoperational period. Because the child is never required by his own reasoning to question his thinking or validate his concepts, intellectual development is restricted at that time. Egocentrism acts to inhibit the process of accommodation. Egocentrism acts to maintain the structural status quo. There is a tendency to assimilate rather than accommodate. Because the child does not question his own thinking, schemata are less likely to change through accommodation. While egocentrism in one sense limits cognitive development during the preoperational period, it is an essential and natural part of the period and of the initial use of any newly acquired cognitive characteristic.

Transformation

Another characteristic of the preoperational child's thinking is his inability to attend to transformations. The child, while observing a sequence of changes or successive states, focuses exclusively on the *elements* in the sequence, or the successive states, rather than on the *transformation* by which one state is changed to another. He does not focus on the process of transformation from an original state to a final state, but restricts his attention to each inbetween state when it occurs. He moves from a particular perceptual event to a particular perceptual event, but cannot integrate a series of events in terms of any beginning-end relationships. His thought is neither inductive nor deductive, but transductive.

If a pencil is held upright (as in Fig. 1) and allowed to fall, it passes from an original state (vertical) to a final state (horizontal), and through a series of successive states. Preoperational children, after viewing the pencil fall, typically cannot draw or otherwise reproduce the successive steps. They cannot attend to or reconstruct the transformation. They usually reproduce only the initial and final positions the pencil assumes.

Figure 1

A second example of the transformation problem is seen in a child walking through the woods. At different points he sees snails (different snails each time). The child cannot tell whether they are all the same snail or different snails. Each snail is viewed in isolation from the previous snails. The child cannot reconstruct the *transformation* from event to event (snail to snail).

The inability of the preoperational child to follow transformations inhibits the development of logic in thought. Since the child is not aware of the relationship between events and all this can mean, comparisons between states of events are always incomplete.

Centration

Another characteristic of preoperational thought is what Piaget calls *centration*. When the child is presented with a visual stimulus, he tends to *center* or fix his attention on a limited perceptual aspect of the stimulus. The child seems unable to "explore" all aspects of the stimulus, or *decenter* his visual inspection. As a result, the child when centering tends to assimilate only the superficial aspects of an event. Any cognitive activity seems to be dominated by the perceptual aspects. Perceptual evaluations dominate the cognitive evaluation (in the preoperational child), much in the same way as they did in the direct action of the sensorimotor child.

If a child is asked to compare two rows of like objects in which one row contains 9 objects and the other, a longer row, contains only 7 objects (spread farther apart), the child of 4 or 5 years will typically select the perceptually longer row as having "more" objects. This will occur even when the child "knows" cognitively that 9 is more than 7. Perceptual evaluation dominates cognitive evaluation.

The child tends to center on perceptual aspects of objects. It is only with time and experience that the child becomes able to *decenter* and evaluate perceptual events in a coordinated way with cognitions. After 6 to 7 years children reach the point where cognitions assume their proper position with respect to perceptions in thought.

Reversibility

Reversibility is the most clearly defined characteristic of intelligence according to Piaget (1963, p. 41). If thought is reversible, it can follow the line of reasoning back to where it started. A child without reversible thought is shown two equal-length rows of 8 coins each. He agrees that each row has the same number of coins. One of the rows is lengthened. The child no longer agrees that there are the same number of coins in each row. Part of the child's problem is that he is not able to *reverse* the act of lengthening. He cannot maintain the equivalence of number in the face of perceptual change. Only when actions become reversible will the child be able to solve such problems. The inability to reverse operations is seen in all cognitive activity of the preoperational child.

Preoperational thought retains much of the rigidity of sensori-motor thought even while surpassing it in quality. It is slow, plodding, inflexible, and dominated by perceptions. As such it remains irreversible. The attainment of reversible operations is extremely difficult for the child. This is reasonable if one considers that *all* sensori-motor operations are irreversible by definition. Once a motor act is committed, it cannot be reversed. In much the same way perceptions cannot be reversed. Thus representational acts, which are based on prior sensori-motor patterns and perceptions, must develop reversibility without any prior patterns to follow (Ibid., p. 41).

Piaget's concepts of egocentrism, centration, transformation, and reversibility are closely related. Early preoperational thought is dominated by each of them. As cognitive development proceeds, these characteristics gradually subside in unison. A deterioration in egocentrism permits (requires) the child to decenter more and attend to simple transformations. All this in turn makes thought more reversible.

CONSERVATION

The characteristics of preoperational thought described function as obstacles to logical thought. Nonetheless they are necessary for the development of logical thought and occur naturally. They are most clearly seen in what have come to be called conservation problems. Conservation is the conceptualization (schematization) that the amount or quantity of a matter stays the same regardless of any changes in shape or position. For example, if we have a row of 8 pennies, and we move the pennies farther apart in the row, we still have 8 pennies. That is, the number of pennies does not change when a change is made in another, irrelevant, dimension (in this case, the length of the row). An awareness of the number invariance would imply ability to conserve number and that corresponding schemata have developed. Lack of this awareness implies lack of number conservation, and that corresponding schemata have not developed. This level of conservation ability is a measure of the type of intellectual structures the child has developed. During the preoperational period, children typically cannot conserve; that is, they cannot hold one dimension invariant in the face of changes in other dimensions. By the end of the preoperational period (age 7) some conservation structures are usually developed.

The development from non-conservation to conservation is a gradual one. As with all other changes in cognitive structures (schemata), the change is largely a function of the actions (cognitive and sensori-motor) of the child. According to Piaget, conservation structures cannot be induced through direct instruction (teaching) or reinforcement techniques. Experience is the key. Conservation of number, area, and volume problems will be presented, followed by a discussion of some of the research that has been done on children's concepts of conservation.

Conservation of Number

If a 4- to 5-year-old is presented with a row of checkers and asked to construct a row that is the same, he typically constructs a row of the same length, but his row may not correspond in the number of elements to the model. The typical construction proceeds by placing two checkers, one opposite each of the end checkers in the model, and then

filling in a number of checkers without one-to-one correspondence. If there is correspondence, it is by accident
(Piaget, 1967, p. 31).

The 5- to 6-year-old is usually a little more systematic.
When he is asked to perform the same conservation task,
he uses one-to-one correspondence and makes each row
equal in number and length to the model. But, if the child
sees one row lengthened (transformed as in Fig. 2) without
any change in the number of elements, the child declares
they are no longer equivalent. This is frequently true even
if he counts the elements in each row. The preoperational
child holds that the rows are equivalent only as long as
there is visual correspondence in the length of arrays (Ibid.,
p. 31).

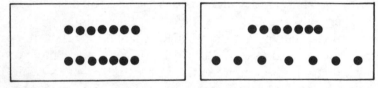

Figure 2

The typical child of 5 or 6 does not conserve number. He
cannot see that number of elements in a series does not
change in the face of other perceptual changes. What has
happened (according to Piagetian theory) is that after a
transformation the child makes a perceptual response, instead of a cognitive response. In terms of previous notions
of *centration*, the child focuses or centers on one aspect of
the event—the length of the rows—and ignores other salient
aspects of which he is cognitively aware: the number of
objects. Also, the child does not focus on the *transformation* of stimulus arrays, but focuses on each successive

state as if it were independent of the previous states. Thus, the child, because of his inability to decenter and focus on the transformation, typically ends up making a perceptual response. Unable to *reverse* the changes that he has seen occur, he resorts to a perceptual response. The child is, in this respect, "perception bound." When confronted with a problem where cognitive and perceptual solutions conflict, the child makes decisions based on the perceptual cues.

Around the age of 6 or 7 the child learns to conserve number. Concurrently he *decenters* his perceptions, attends to the *transformations*, and *reverses* operations.

Conservation of Area

A second type of conservation problem reflects the child's concepts of *area*. This can be demonstrated by the cows-in-the-field problem (Piaget, Inhelder, and Szeminska, 1960, p. 262). Two sheets of green paper (same size) are placed before the child, and a cow (toy or paper cutout) is placed in each field as in Fig. 3a. Several blocks of the same size are kept on hand to represent buildings. It is explained to the child that there are two fields of grass and a cow in each field. The child is asked; "Which cow has more grass to eat?" Typically, the response will be that both cows have the same amount of grass to eat. Once visual equivalence of area is established, the child is shown a barn (block) being placed in each field, and the question is repeated: "Which cow has more grass to eat now?" Again, the response is typically that they both have the same amount of grass. A second block is placed in each field (Fig. 3b); but in the first field, the second block is placed away from the first, and in the other field the second block is placed adjacent to the first. The question is repeated: "Which cow has more grass to eat now?" The

Figure 3a

Figure 3b

child who cannot conserve typically says that the cow in the second field (blocks adjacent) has more grass to eat. The child who can conserve says that they both have the same amount to eat. The extension of this problem by more barn placements can be varied to check the reliability of the conservation or non-conservation responses.

Again, the non-conserving preoperational child has made a perceptual response. The second field looks like it has less buildings (because they are attached) than the first field. The child is not able to *decenter* and attend to all the salient aspects of the event, nor does he follow the *transformations* that have taken place. Each new placement is independent of the previous. Thus, as with conservation of number problems, the preoperational child fails to conserve. Not until ages 7 to 8 is conservation of area usually attained.

Conservation of Volume

A third type of problem is the conservation of volume problem. The preoperational child's inability to conserve volume can usually be shown with the following task. The child is presented with two containers of equal size and shape as in Fig. 4. The child is asked to compare the

Figure 4

amount of liquid in the two containers. A few drops are added to one, if necessary, to establish visual equivalence of volume. When equivalence is attained, the liquid from one of the glasses is poured into a taller and thinner glass (or shorter and wider glass), and the child is again asked to compare the two containers holding liquid. The typical preoperational child no longer sees the two containers as equivalent in volume and declares that one or the other (usually the taller and thinner container) has more liquid. This is clearly a non-conservation response. If the liquid is then poured back into the original container, visual equivalence is usually achieved again for the child, though not because the child conserves.

As in the previous conservation problems, the preoperational child typically does not attend to all aspects of the *transformation* that he sees. He *centers* on the perceptual aspects of the problem. Because the taller cylinder looks larger, it must contain more liquid. Reasoning is not logical. Reversibility is not present. It is not until concrete operations (ages 7 to 11) that volume conservation is usually present.[1]

The preceding conservation problems illustrate but do not begin to exhaust the phenomenon of conservation. Qualitative differences in the logical thought of the child manifest themselves in *all* aspects of their thinking. A change along one dimension always seems to imply changes in other dimensions for the preoperational child. The reverse is true for his older counterparts who develop schemata permitting conservation.

---

[1] Volume problems of the above type are usually solved after 7 or 8. More sophisticated volume conservation problems, such as those requiring the measurement of displaced water when an object is immersed, are not solved until about age 12 [Piaget and Inhelder, 1969, p. 98].

The picture of conservation presented here is somewhat oversimplified. The child does not develop conservation schemata overnight in an all or nothing manner. Conservation concepts are acquired slowly after much experience and subsequent assimilation and accommodation. Qualitatively new patterns of responses are interpreted by Piaget to reflect newly formed schemata (cognitive structures).

The acquisition of schemata permitting conservation does not take place at the same time in all areas. The application of conservation principles to different types of problems usually follows a sequence. Conservation of number is usually attained before other conservation skills, and conservation of volume is usually attained last. The structures permitting conservation are typically acquired at the following ages:

number	5-6
substance (mass)	7-8
area	7-8
weight	9-10
volume	11-12

Such a developmental sequence suggests that the ability to conserve volume always implies the ability to conserve weight, area, substance, and number. Each new type of conservation always implies that previous levels in the sequence have been attained.

RESEARCH ON CONSERVATION LEARNING

Piaget's conceptualizations indicate that conservation concepts are acquired in a sequence. Research on the sequential development of conservation concepts is also found in the literature and these studies generally confirm Piaget's findings. Urgiris (1968) found that of 120 subjects between the ages of 7 and 11, 112 evidenced conservation of substance, weight, and volume in the order Piaget describes. Elkind (*Children's Discovery of the Conservation of Mass, Weight, and Volume, 1961*) tested 175 children in kindergarten to grade six on conservation of mass, weight, and volume. The results of his study confirmed Piaget's findings with respect to the age at which conservation concepts are attained and with respect to the order in which they are attained. Another study by Elkind (*Quality Conceptions in Junior and Senior High School Students, 1961*) involving problems in conservation of mass, weight, and volume found the sequence suggested by Piaget in 469 junior and senior high school students. These studies confirm Piaget's belief that conservation concepts are attained in an invariant sequence.

A second set of studies deals with the effects of schooling, direct instruction, and reinforcement techniques on the acquisition of conservation skills. Most of these studies suggest that direct teaching does not produce permanent conservation learning in preoperational children.

Gruen (1965) unsuccessfully used training procedures to try to induce conservation of number skills in 45 kinder garten children. Wohlwill and Lowe (1962) found that continued reinforced practice in conservation of number was ineffective in improving conservation responses. Wallach, Wall, and Anderson (1967), using 56 first-graders, examined the effect of reversibility training and addition and subtraction experience on conservation of number. No effect due to the addition and subtraction training was noted. Reversibility training was reported to affect conservation responses. Kohlberg (1968) found that a special Montessori schooling program for children over a nine-month period raised I.Q. test scores but did not significantly affect performance on conservation tasks. These studies all add credence to Piaget's belief that cognitive structures (schemata) cannot be induced directly as a substitute for general experience.

Along similar lines, a number of studies have been done on the conservation ability of children who have not had formal schooling. Unschooled children typically evolve conservation concepts at about the same age as schooled children in most cultures. Mermelstein and Shulman (1967) examined the conservation responses on a number of conservation tasks of 6- and 9-year-old Negro children in Prince Edward County, Virginia, who had not attended school for four years. These responses were compared with the responses on the same tasks of Northern Negro children who had attended school. No significant differences between the groups were found. Goodnow and Bethon (1966), in a study of Hong Kong children, similarly found no differences between the performance of unschooled and schooled children of comparable intelligence on various conservation tasks. As in other studies, all tasks showed a close relation to the mental age of children.

In contrast with the preceding studies, Greenfield (1966) found that unschooled Senegalese children from bush areas were significantly retarded in conservation ability when compared with city and bush children that had had schooling.

These few studies suggest that formal schooling, or lack of it, does not usually influence conservation ability, but that conservation abilities appear at the same age in schooled and unschooled subjects. According to Piaget's theory, instruction (schooling) rarely leads directly to the formation of a stable schemata for conservation. Qualitative changes in schemata can come about only with considerable general experience which children usually have regardless of whether they go to school or not. Intellectual structures (schemata) cannot be erected on demand but are contingent on a background of general experience.[2]

Piaget contends that conservation abilities evolve "naturally" out of the experiences most children have. Children tend to develop conservation abilities at about the same age, and tend to develop different conservation operations in an invariant sequence. In most cultures, children without formal schooling attain conservation as readily as children with schooling, and direct teaching of conservation skills to preoperational children is not generally successful.

The interpretation of these findings according to Piagetian theory is that conservation abilities will not emerge until cognitive structures (schemata) evolve that make true conservation responses possible. Changes in schemata come about only after considerable assimilation and accommodation of experience. The child must attain reversibility, learn to decenter perceptions, and follow transformations. He must become less egocentric and learn to question his thinking. These changes all come about gradually and are prerequisites to the development of the schemata permitting conservation.

SUMMARY OF THE PREOPERATIONAL PERIOD

Qualitatively the thought of the preoperational child is an advance over the thought of the sensori-motor child. It

---

[2] This should not be interpreted to mean that children learn regardless of whether they go to school. It means only that cognitive structures (schemata) will evolve in most cases regardless of whether children go to school or not. Chapter eight deals with this in more detail.

is no longer primarily restricted to immediate perceptual and motor events. Thought is truly representational (symbolic) and behavior sequences can be played out in the head rather than only in real physical events.

The preoperational period is marked by some dramatic attainments. Language is acquired very rapidly between the ages of 2 and 4. Behavior in the early part of the period is largely egocentric and non-social. These characteristics become less dominant as the period proceeds and by age 6 or 7 children's conversations become largely communicative and social.

While preoperational thought is an advance over sensori-motor thought, it is restricted in many respects. The child is unable to reverse operations, he cannot follow transformations; perceptions tend to be centered, and the child is egocentric. These characteristics make for slow, concrete, and restricted thought. During this period thought is still largely under the control of the immediate and the perceptual, as is seen in the typical preoperational child's inability to solve conservation problems.

Cognitive development is not arrested from ages 2 to 7. Rather, it moves steadily along, assimilation and accommodation resulting in the constant evolution of new and improved cognitive machinery (schemata). The preoperational child's behavior is initially like that of the sensori-motor child. By age 7 there is little resemblance.

Chapter Five

Period of Concrete Operations

During the period of concrete operations (ages 7 to 11), the child's reasoning processes become logical. He develops what Piaget calls *logical operations*. That is, the child evolves logical thought processes (operations) that can be applied to concrete problems. Unlike the preoperational child, the concrete operational child has no trouble solving the conservation problems. When faced with a discrepancy between thought and perception, as in conservation problems, the concrete operational child makes cognitive and logical decisions as opposed to perceptual decisions. The concrete operational child is no longer perception-bound. He becomes able, between the ages of 7 and 11, to do all the cognitive operations that limit the intellectual activity of the preoperational child. He *decenters* his perceptions and attends to *transformations*. Most important, the concrete operational child attains *reversibility* of operations. In addition, cooperative, nonegocentric communication evolves. The child for the first time becomes a truly social being.

The quality of concrete operational thought surpasses that of preoperational thought. Schemata for the operations of seriation and classification appear. Improved concepts of causality, space, time, and speed evolve. In essence, the concrete operational child attains a level of intellectual activity that is superior in all respects to that of the preoperational child.

While the concrete operational child evolves a functional use of logic not evidenced in the behavior of younger children, he does not attain the highest level of use of logical operations. Here the term *concrete* (as in concrete operations) is significant. While the child clearly evolves logical operations, these operations (reversibility, classification, etc.) are only useful to him in solving problems involving concrete (real, observable) objects and events. For the most part, the child cannot yet apply his logic to problems that are hypothetical or purely verbal. If the concrete operational child is presented with a purely verbal problem, he is typically unable to solve it correctly. If the same problem is presented in terms of real objects, the child can apply his logical operations and solve the problem. Thus, the concrete operational period can be viewed as providing a transition between pre-logical (preoperational) thought and the completely logical thought of the older child.

HOW CONCRETE OPERATIONAL THOUGHT DIFFERS FROM PREOPERATIONAL THOUGHT

The preoperational child's thought is characterized by egocentrism, centration, inability to follow transformations, and inability to reverse operations. These obstacles to logical thought are reflected in the preoperational child's inability to solve conservation problems. In contrast, concrete operational thought is free of all the characteristics that dominated preoperational thought. The typical concrete operational child can solve the conservation problems. His thought is less egocentric, he can decenter his perceptions, he follows transformations, and most important, he can reverse operations. These characteristics will be discussed in the following pages.

Egocentrism and Socialization

The preoperational child's thinking was dominated by egocentrism, an inability to assume the viewpoint of others and a lack of a need to seek validation of his own thoughts. The concrete operational child's thinking is not egocentric in this respect. He is aware that others can come to conclusions that are different from his, and as a consequence he comes to seek validation of his thoughts. In this respect the concrete operational child is liberated from the intellectual egocentrism of the previous period.

Liberation from egocentrism, according to Piaget, comes about primarily through social interaction with peers.[1] During social (conceptual) interaction with peers, the child is forced to seek verification of his ideas. Piaget (1928) writes:

> What then gives rise to the need for verification? Surely it must be the shock of our thoughts coming into contact with that of others, which produces doubt and the desire to prove . . . The social need to share the thoughts of others and to communicate our own with success is at the root of our need for verification. Proof is the outcome of argument . . . Argument is, therefore, the backbone of verification [p. 204].

The concrete operational child does not display the egocentrism of thought characteristic of the preoperational

[1] Piaget states that social interaction is one of the variables that facilitates cognitive development. His writings suggest that social interactions are any behaviors (conversations, play, games, etc.) that involve a real interchange between two or more persons. Thus, when language becomes functionally communicative, it is a form of social interaction.

child. At this time his use of language becomes communicative in function. Through social interaction concepts are verified or denied. As has been said previously, the socialization of behavior is a continuous process that begins in early childhood with simple imitations. Social behavior, by its very nature, is an important form of accommodation. Coming to look at something from another's viewpoint, questioning one's reasoning, and seeking validation from others are all essentially acts of accommodation.

The process of socialization is progressive rather than regressive (Piaget and Inhelder, 1969, p. 117). That is, the child's behavior is always becoming more social. Children's behaviors in games with rules become increasingly social. In the games of marbles, after the age of 7 or so, behaviors are well structured with common adherence to rules and a collective spirit of honest competition. Prior to 7 years, each child plays to have fun and everyone can win. True cooperation and competition (social behavior) do not appear before the concrete operations (Ibid., p. 119).

With the arrival of concrete operations, language becomes less egocentric. Collective monologues, characteristic of children's speech before 6 or 7 years, are largely absent after that time. Children exchange information with each other in their conversations and learn to speak from the viewpoint of others.

Centration

The preoperational child's thinking is characterized by centration or centering. Perceptions of events tend to center on a single perceptual characteristic of a stimulus and to not take into account all the salient features of the stimulus. Thus, in conservation of number problems, preoperational children tend to center on the length of stimulus configurations.

The concrete operational child's thinking is not characterized by centering. Concrete thought becomes decentered, taking into account all the salient features of objects. Decentering is one of the abilities found in concrete thought that permits conservation.

Transformations

The preoperational child was unable to coordinate and focus on the successive steps in a transformation. Each step in a transformation was viewed as independent of each successive step. There was no awareness or attention paid to the sequence or transformation involved.

The concrete operational child attains a functional understanding of transformations. He can solve problems involving transformations and is aware of and understands the relationship between successive steps.

Reversibility

Preoperational thought lacks reversibility. Concrete operational thought is reversible. The difference between the two levels of thought can be seen in the following illustration from Piaget (1967, p. 31). A child is shown three balls of the same size, each of a different color (A, B, C). The balls are placed in a cylinder in the order A, B, C. The preoperational child correctly predicts that they will exit from the bottom of the cylinder in the same order, A, B, C. Once more the balls are in the cylinder in the same order. Then the cylinder is rotated 180 degrees. The preoperational child continues to predict that the balls will exit from the bottom of the tube in the same order as before, A, B, C. He is surprised when they exit in the order C, B, A. This is an example of the inability of preoperational thought to reverse operations. The concrete operational child has no trouble with the above problem.

He can reverse the inversion and make the appropriate deduction. In this way concrete thought is reversible.

Conservation

The hallmark of preoperational thought is the inability of the child to conserve. With the attainment of concrete operations, the ability to solve conservation problems emerges. The related abilities to decenter, to follow transformations, and to reverse operations are all instrumental in developing conservation skills. The child becomes able to solve the conservation of number problems around age 6 or 7. Conservation of area and mass problems are usually solved by age 7 or 8. Conservation of volume problems (measurement of displaced water when an object is immersed) are not solved correctly until age 11 or 12.

LOGICAL OPERATIONS

Cognitively, the most important development of the concrete operational period is the attainment of logical operations. Logical operations are internalized cognitive actions that permit the child to arrive at conclusions that are "logical." These actions are directed by cognitive activity rather than being dominated by perceptions. Logical operations evolve, as do all cognitive structures, out of prior structures as a function of assimilation and accommodation. Logical operations are means of organizing experience (schemata) that are superior to prior organization.

According to Piaget, an operation always has four characteristics. It is an action that can be internalized or carried out in thought as well as materially. It is reversible. An operation always supposes some conservation, some invariance. And an operation never exists alone but is always related to a system of operations (Piaget, 1970, p. 21-22).

Operations become truly logical during the concrete operational period. Previous operations (preoperational period) were pre-logical, never meeting all the above criteria. One logical operation already discussed is reversibility. Two other operations are seriation and classification.

Seriation

A cognitive operation acquired during the concrete operational period is seriation, the ability to mentally arrange elements according to increasing or decreasing size. If a preoperational child (before 6 or 7 years) is shown two sticks of slightly different lengths (A and B), he can compare them and visually determine that A is shorter than B. If he is then shown sticks B and C (where B is shorter than C) while A is hidden from view, he can again visually determine that B is less than C. If the child is then asked to compare A to C, while A is still hidden, he cannot make the appropriate deduction (A < B, B < C, so A < C). The child typically requests to see A and C together so he can compare them. Such responses indicate the preoperational child cannot mentally order events in a series. He cannot construct the necessary mental scale to order objects or events.

Seriation learning, like conservation learning, typically occurs at different ages in an invariant sequence. The child first learns to seriate length (as in the above problem) around age 7, the beginning of concrete operations. Seriation of weight (seriation of objects of the same size but different weight) is usually attained around age 9. Similarly, seriation of volume is not arrived at until age 12 or so (Piaget, 1967, p. 51). As can be seen, the ability to seriate or order objects or events along a particular dimension (length, weight, volume), occurs at about the same time as conservation skills emerge with respect to the same dimension.

In a manner analogous to the development of seriation concepts, the child develops concepts of equivalence (A = B; B = C; therefore A = C). Length, weight, and volume equivalences are attained at about the same time as concepts of seriation and conservation with respect to each dimension. Equivalence of length is attained before equivalence of volume (Ibid., p. 51).

Classification

Classification is another logical operation that becomes operative during the concrete operational period. Prior to that period children have certain problems in classifying objects and events and relating these classifications. The following example from Piaget (*The Child's Conception of Number*, 1952) illustrates the development of operations involved in the comparison of classes. A child is shown a box containing 20 wooden beads, 18 of which are brown; the other 2 white. The child is told to examine the beads and put the brown beads in a separate box. When this is properly accomplished, it indicates the child has the classification "brown." The same procedure is used to establish

Figure 5

the child's ability to classify according to "white" and "wooden." Most children can make these simple classifications by age 4. Once the classes of brown, white, and wooden have been established, the child is asked, "Are there more wooden beads or more brown beads?"

At the preoperational level most children respond that there are more brown beads than wooden beads. At the concrete operational level (after age 7), most children respond that there are more wooden beads than brown beads. The preoperational child cannot perform the *logical operation* of the addition of classes, while the concrete operational child can. The concrete operational child can simultaneously take into consideration two kinds of classes. He can perform the addition of classes and he can reverse the process. After age 8 or so the typical child understands the relationship between an included class (subclass) and an entire class. The preoperational child seems to be able to classify the beads along only one dimension at a time. He cannot compare the beads as both wooden and white, or both wooden and brown. An apparent perceptual difference exists between the beads in the problem, and the preoperational child makes a perceptual response. As in conservation problems, the preoperational child *centers* on one dimension (color) and disregards the common wooden characteristics of all the beads.

A number of experimenters have studied the development of classification behaviors in children. Kofsky (1966) did an analysis of eleven different classification tasks with children from ages 4 to 9. These tasks were all derived from Piaget's work. The observed order of task difficulty reported by Kofsky was in accord with the theoretical expectations derived from Piaget's work. A significant correlation between the ages of the children studied and the number of tasks they completed successfully was found (r = .86, p. < .01). Ability to perform classifications was related to age. These results tend to confirm Piaget's notions with respect to classifications. Kofsky also conducted an analysis (scalogram) of the sequence in which classifications theoretically were expected to occur. The results of the analysis were partially confirming. Some children passed theoretically difficult tasks while not being able to pass easier tasks.

By now it should be clear to the reader that Piaget conceptualizes cognitive development as occurring not in isolation, but in all areas at the same time. A cognitive advance in one area has effects in other areas. With this in mind, the concrete operational child's concepts of causality, time, and speed will be discussed.

Causality

Children's concepts of causality develop as do other concepts. Development of causal concepts during the sensorimotor period was illustrated in Chapter Three. Piaget and Inhelder (1969) investigated children's concepts of causality in the following problem situation:

> . . . we once asked children from five to twelve what happens after lumps of sugar are dissolved in a glass of water. For children up to about seven, the dissolved sugar disappears and its taste vanishes like a mere odor; for children seven to eight its substance is retained without either its weight or its volume. After nine or ten, conservation of weight is present, and after eleven or twelve, there is also conservation of volume (recognizable in the fact that the level of water, which is slightly raised when the sugar is added, does not return to its initial level after the sugar is dissolved) [p. 112].

As illustrated in the above example, children's causal concepts develop during the concrete operational period.

Qualitative changes in structures (schemata) are reflected in the development.

Time and Speed

Piaget contends that children do not understand the relationship between time and speed (velocity = speed/time) until ages 10 or 11 (Piaget and Inhelder, 1969, p. 103). Prior to this age an object is considered to travel faster than another object only if it overtakes it while moving. The preoperational child, when comparing the speeds of two objects, usually considers only the points of arrival, and does not consider starting points and subsequent velocity or paths followed (Ibid., p. 108). Consider the following example. Two cars leave point A in Fig. 6 at the

Figure 6

same time. They both arrive at B at the same time but traverse different routes (1 and 2). After viewing this problem, observing the movement of the cars, the preoperational child reports both cars traveled at the same speed. It is not until after age 8 or so, according to Piaget, that a ratio concept of speed in terms of the relationship between time and distance traveled begins to evolve.

The concrete operational child's concepts of time and speed are superior to those of the preoperational child. Not until the period of concrete operations do reliable concepts appear.

SUMMARY OF THE PERIOD OF CONCRETE OPERATIONS

The period of concrete operations serves as a transition period between preoperational thought and formal (logical) thought. During this period the child attains the use of logical operations for the first time. Thought is no longer dominated by perceptions, the child being able to logically solve concrete problems.

The concrete operational child is not egocentric in his thought. He can assume the viewpoints of others and his language is social and communicative. He can decenter his perceptions and attend to transformations. All these new characteristics of thought are reflected in his ability to solve the conservation problems that he was previously unable to solve. An important attainment is reversibility, an essential quality in all operations. Two operations developed during this period are seriation and classification.

While concrete thought is clearly superior to preoperational thought, it remains inferior to the thought of the older child (over 11 or 12). The concrete operational child can use logical operations to solve problems involving "concrete" objects and events. He cannot solve hypothetical problems, problems that are entirely verbal, and some problems requiring more complex operations. Only with the attainment of formal thought will the development of cognitive structures be complete.

Chapter Six

The Period of Formal Operations

During the period of formal operations, approximately ages 11 to 15 years, the child develops the ability to solve all classes of problems that can be solved through logical operations. According to Piaget, the child's cognitive structures reach maturity during this period. That is, his potential in terms of quality of thought (as compared to the potential of adult thought) is at its maximum when formal operations are achieved. After this period there are no further structural improvements in the cognitive apparatus (schemata). The adolescent with formal operations typically has the cognitive *structural* equipment to think "as well as" adults. This does not mean that adolescent (formal) thought is necessarily "as good as" adult thought in a particular instance, only that the attainment of formal operations means a new potentiality has been achieved.

Assimilation and accommodation continue throughout life to produce changes in schemata. From the end of the period of formal operations, changes in thought abilities are quantitative and no longer qualitative with respect to logical operations and structure. Structures of intelligence do not improve after this period. Content and function of intelligence may improve. This is not meant to imply that the use of thought cannot or does not improve after adolescence. The content and function (use to which thought is put) of thought are free to vary and improve after this period, which in part helps to explain some of the classical differences between adolescent thought and adult thought (see Chapter Seven).

HOW FORMAL OPERATIONS DIFFER FROM CONCRETE OPERATIONS

Functionally, formal thought and concrete thought are the same. They both employ logical operations. The major difference between the two types of thought is the much larger range of application of logical operations available to the child with formal thought. Concrete thought is limited to solving tangible problems of the present. Concrete operational children cannot deal with complex verbal problems, hypothetical problems, or those involving the future. To this extent, the concrete operational child is not completely free of his perceptions. In contrast, the child with formal operations can deal with all classes of problems, the present, past, and future, the hypothetical, and the verbal. Thus, the child with formal operations is liberated from the content of problems.

The concrete operational child must deal with each problem in isolation. Operations are not coordinated. The child cannot integrate his solutions by means of general theories. The child with formal operations can employ theories in the solution of many problems in an integrated manner. Several operations can be brought to bear on a single problem.

In addition, formal operations are characterized by scientific reasoning, hypothesis building (and testing), and they reflect a true understanding of causation. For the first time the child can operate on the logic of an argument (problem) independent of its content. He is aware that logically derived conclusions have a validity independent of factual truth. While both concrete thought and formal thought have much in common, they are clearly different. The concrete operational child lacks the range and power of thought of his older counterpart.

CHARACTERISTICS OF FORMAL OPERATIONS

Formal thought arises out of concrete operations in the same way that each new level of thought incorporates and modifies prior thought. During the period of formal operations the child is better able to organize data, reason scientifically, and generate hypotheses. These characteristics of thought are seen in a number of problems that are easily solved with formal operations but are impossible to solve with concrete operations. Such problems are those involving: combinatorial thought, complex verbal problems, hypothetical problems, proportions, and conservation of movement. Examples of each of these are presented next.

Combinatorial Thought

Piaget and Inhelder (1969) describe the difference between concrete and formal thought in a problem involving combinatorial thought. A child is presented with five jars containing colorless liquids. The combination of three of the liquids (1, 3, 5) produces a yellow color. The other two jars contain a bleaching agent or water. The child is shown the colored liquid that can be produced but he does not see how it is obtained. When children are asked to produce the yellow color, those of 7 to 11 years typically proceed by combining two liquids at a time. After combining pairs, the systematic nature of their searching stops.

They may then mix all five together (which does not produce a yellow color). After the age of 12 children typically test all possible combinations of one, two, and three liquids until the yellow solution is reached (p. 134).

The concrete operational child's explorations are systematic up to a certain point, but he does not explore all possible combinations. In contrast, the child with formal operations explores all possible solutions. Again, the qualitative difference between concrete and formal thought is illustrated.

Verbal Problems

Children without formal operations are usually not able to solve the following verbal problem. The problem is derived from one of Burt's tests that was standardized by Piaget early in his career.

> Edith is fairer than Susan; Edith is darker than Lilly; Who is the darkest of the three? (Piaget, 1968, p. 162).

Children under the age of 12 have trouble solving this problem. Their reasoning is similar to that of the younger child in the previous problem of serializing sticks. Not until age 12 or later can children usually do with verbal problems what they learned to do with concrete problems around age 7 (Ibid., p. 149).

Hypothetical Problems

The child with formal operations can reason on the basis of assumption while children with concrete thought cannot. The older child can operate on the logic of an argument independently of its content. He is aware that conclusions logically derived from assumptions have a validity that is independent of their factual truth.

If a logical argument is prefixed by the statement, "Suppose coal is white . . .,"[1] the concrete operational child, when asked to solve the logical problem, declares that coal is black and that he cannot answer the question. Presented with the same problem, the child with formal operations readily accepts the assumption that coal is white and proceeds with the logic of the argument. The older child can extract the structure of the argument from its content and submit the structure (alone) to logical analysis. The concrete operational child typically cannot deal with an argument independent of its content. Coal is black and the problem is unsolvable.

Proportion

The development of children's concepts of proportion can be viewed in their actions with a seesaw balance of the type in Figure 7.[2] Before the age of 7 children have difficulty equalizing weights on a balance. They are aware that a balance is possible, but their attempts to attain it are always successive trial-and-error corrections. Compensation on the balance is never systematic. After age 7 (concrete operations) children discover a small weight can balance a larger weight by placing it farther from the fulcrum than the larger weight. They learn to equalize weight and length in a systematic manner. But they do not coordinate the two functions of weight and length as a proportion.

Around age 13 comprehension of the proportion principle ($W/L = 2W/2L$) occurs when the child becomes aware that an increase in weight on one side of the fulcrum can

---

[1] Adapted from Elkind (1967).

[2] The discussion of proportion is based on Piaget and Inhelder's book, *The Growth of Logical Thinking from Childhood to Adolescence*, 1958, pp. 164-181.

Figure 7

be compensated for by an increase in distance from the fulcrum on the other side. Thus the development of the child's conception of proportion is consistent with his general conceptual development in that qualitative differences in schemata of proportion are found at different periods.

Conservation of Movement; the Pendulum Problem

A pendulum can be made to swing faster or slower by adjusting the length of the string holding it (the shorter the string the faster the movement). When asked to adjust the speed of a pendulum, concrete operational children typically insist on adjusting the weight of the pendulum. If they adjust the length of the string, they usually adjust the weight of the pendulum at the same time. They insist on attributing any change in the speed of the pendulum to the adjustment in the weight. Concrete operational children have difficulty separating the variables of weight and length.

During the period of formal operations, children learn to separate weight and length in the pendulum problem. By age 15, subjects are usually aware that the length of the string is the important variable affecting the speed of the pendulum (Inhelder and Piaget, 1958, pp. 67-79).

SUMMARY OF THE PERIOD OF FORMAL OPERATIONS

The period of formal operations is the culmination of the development of cognitive structures. Schemata typically reach maximum *qualitative* development by about age 15. The adolescent is able to think logically in relation to all classes of problems. He can solve hypothetical problems, verbal problems, and he can use scientific reasoning. Formal operations evolve out of concrete operations. The processes of assimilation and accommodation constantly modify cognitive structures through the period of formal operations. Each structural change incorporates and improves upon previous structures. The process of development of schemata begins at birth and culminates in adolescence.

Chapter Seven

Cognitive Development
and Adolescence[1]

Adolescent behavior has always been a matter of concern to parents, educators, and psychologists. Many theorists have tried to account for the unique characteristics of the adolescent period. Psychoanalytic theory (Freud, 1946; Erickson, 1959) offers a rationalization for affective and social aspects of adolescent behavior, though there has been little supporting research for this position. Behaviorists by and large have avoided the topic of adolescence. While adolescence has received considerable attention in educational and psychological literature, little of this attention has been concerned with the intellectual development of the older child.

The aspect of Piaget's work that has probably been most neglected is that which attempts to account for the uniqueness of adolescent thought and behavior. While Piaget does not attempt to explain all adolescent behavior, he does provide an important link between cognitive development and general behavior. It is unfortunate (in the

---

[1] For present purposes, adolescence will be thought of as roughly from 15 to 18 years. The adolescent is assumed to have developed formal operations.

opinion of the writer) that Piaget's thoughts on this topic have not attracted more interest and attention.

Piaget's explanation of adolescent behavior is consistent with the rest of his theory. He sees the unique character- istics of adolescent thought and personality as a normal outgrowth of development. That is, much of adolescent thought and behavior can be explained by prior develop- ment. In this respect the development of cognitive struc- tures before and during adolescence helps to account for the characteristics of behavior during the age period.

The adolescent is typically one who has entered the pe- riod of formal operations and is developing, or has de- veloped, the cognitive skills of that period. Logical opera- tions permit the child to solve a wide range of logical problems. At this point the qualitative development of cognitive structures is presumed complete. The typical adolescent has the mental apparatus required to solve prob- lems logically as well as adults can. Why then does the adolescent "think differently" from the adult?

Piaget believes the characteristics of adolescent thought that make him unique are in large measure due to the child's level of cognitive development and his accom- panying *egocentrism* of thought.

EGOCENTRISM AND ADOLESCENCE

Egocentrism is the constant companion of cognitive development. At each new stage of mental growth, the child's inability to differentiate assumes a unique form and is expressed in a novel set of behaviors. Thus, one of the characteristics of thought associated with all newly ac- quired cognitive structures is egocentrism. This can be thought of as a negative byproduct of mental development which, in a sense, distorts the initial use of newly acquired cognitive structures. Each period of development finds egocentrism manifest in a unique form.

During the sensori-motor period (0-2 years) the child is egocentric in the sense that he cannot differentiate between other objects and himself as an object, nor between objects and his sensory impressions. He is the center of his world. With development during the period, this type of egocentrism subsides. It disappears by the time the child becomes able to internally represent objects and events. The egocentrism of the preoperational period (2 to 7 years) is seen in the inability of children to differentiate between their own thoughts and those of others. The child believes his thoughts are always correct. The egocentrism of the preoperational period subsides as social interaction with others (particularly peers) increases. Elkind (1967) suggests the preoperational child is also egocentric in being unable to differentiate between symbols (words) and their referrents. The child of this period is seen to give incomplete verbal descriptions to others, believing that words carry more information than they really do (p. 1025).

During concrete operations (7 to 11 years) the child becomes able to apply logical operations to concrete problems. Egocentrism takes the form of inability to differentiate between perceptual events and mental constructions. The child cannot "think" independently of his perceptions. Hypotheses requiring perceptually untrue assumptions (coal is white) cannot be pursued. Only the attainment of formal operations permits this form of egocentrism to diminish.

As each new plane of cognitive functioning is initially characterized by a type of egocentrism, so too is adolescence. The adolescent, in a sense, becomes possessed with his new-found powers of logical thought. In adolescent thought, the criterion for making judgments becomes what is logical to the adolescent, not always what is realistic. The egocentrism of adolescence is the inability of the child to differentiate between his idealistic thought and the "real" world, The adolescent is emboldened with the egocentric belief in the omnipotence of logical thought. He can think logically about the future and about hypothetical people and events. He feels that the world should submit itself to idealistic (logical) schemes rather than to systems of reality. He does not understand that the world is not always rationally ordered, as he thinks it should be. Inhelder and Piaget (1958) write:

> . . . when the cognitive field is again enlarged by the structuring of formal thought, a . . . form of egocentrism comes into view. This egocentrism is one of the most enduring features of adolescence . . . the adolescent not only tries to adapt his ego to the social environment but, just as emphatically, tries to adjust the environment to his ego . . . The result is a relative failure to distinguish between his point of view . . . and the point of view of the group which he hopes to reform . . . But we believe that, in the egocentrism found in the adolescent, there is more than a simple desire to deviate; rather, it is a manifestation of the phenomenon of lack of differentiation . . . the adolescent goes through a phase in which he attributes an unlimited power to his own thoughts so that the dreams of a glorious future of transforming the world through ideas . . . seems to be not only fantasy but also an effective action which in itself modifies the empirical world [pp. 343-346].

According to Piaget's formulation, to some extent the differences between the thought of adolescents and adults is in part a function of the normal course of cognitive development. Inhelder and Piaget (Ibid.) say:

> We have seen that the principal intellectual characteristics of adolescence stem directly or indirectly from the development

of formal structures. Thus, the latter is the most important
event in the thinking found in this period [p. 347] .

The adolescent becomes involved in an idealistic crisis.
He has the powers of propositional logic, but he cannot
distinguish between the new powers and society applying
it to theories. It might seem that adolescents are doomed
forever to be idealistic social critics. But, as the egocentrism of other periods gradually diminishes, so does the
egocentrism of adolescence. Egocentrism subsides when
the adolescent learns to use his logic effectively in relation
to the reality of life, and not only in relation to life as he
thinks it should be. Inhelder and Piaget (Ibid.) write:

> . . . the focal point of the decentering process is the entrance
> into the occupational world or the beginning of serious profes-
> sional training. The adolescent becomes an adult when he
> undertakes a real job. It is then that he is transformed from an
> idealistic reformer into an achiever. In other words, the job
> leads thinking away from the dangers of formalism back into
> reality. [p. 346]

The adolescent must learn to assume adult (realistic) roles
in the real world. This involves not only cognitive development but also a parallel affective development.

The mental developments of adolescence are essential to
the subsequent development of adult thought, but they do
not ensure adult thought. The implementation of formal
thought in adolescence is initially egocentric. The adolescent does not differentiate between the many possible perspectives. Objectivity of thought with respect to conflict-
ing issues is attained (and egocentrism lost) when the
adolescent assumes adult roles in the real world and can
differentiate the many possible points of view (Ibid.,
p. 345).

Chapter Eight

Summary of Piaget's Theory and Its Implications for Education

What has been presented so far is an introduction to Piaget's theory of cognitive development. The basic elements of his work have been presented, though they have not been examined in detail. A realistic evaluation of Piaget's theory cannot be made if it is based only on the material presented in this book.

The attempt has been made to trace the logical development of the structures of intelligence from birth through adulthood. Hopefully the relationship between early sensori-motor development and later development has been established. Piaget's theory clearly suggests that the path of cognitive development is the same for all people. From his theory, a descriptive outline of cognitive development has emerged.

SUMMARY

During the sensori-motor period (0-2 years) the infant's reflexive behaviors gradually evolve into clearly intelligent behavior. Through maturation and interaction with the environment (assimilation and accommodation), sensori-motor behaviors become increasingly differentiated and progressively evolve into intentional behaviors. The infant

TABLE 2

Summary of the Periods of Cognitive Development

Period	Characteristics of the Period	Major Change of the Period
Sensori-motor (0-2 years)		Development proceeds from reflex acitvity to representation and sensori-motor solutions to problems
Stage 1 (0-1 months)	Reflex activity only No differentiation	
Stage 2 (1-4 months)	Hand-mouth coordination Differentiation via sucking reflex	
Stage 3 (4-8 months)	Hand-eye coordination Repeats unusual events	
Stage 4 (8-12 months)	Coordination of two schemata Object permanence attained	
Stage 5 (12-18 months)	New means through experimentation—follows sequential displacements	
Stage 6 (18-24 months)	Internal representation New means through mental combinations	

Preoperational (2-7 years)	Problems solved through representation—language development (2-4 years) Thought and language both egocentric Cannot solve conservation problems	Development proceeds from sensori-motor representation to pre-logical thought and solutions to problems
Concrete Operational (7-11 years)	Reversability attained Can solve conservation problems—logical operations developed and applied to concrete problems Cannot solve complex verbal problems	Development proceeds from pre-logical thought to logical solutions to concrete problems
Formal operations (11-15 years)	Logically solves all types of problems—thinks scientifically Solves complex verbal problems Cognitive structures mature	Development proceeds from logical solutions to concrete problems to logical solutions to all classes of problems

develops means-end problem solving behavior. Before the age of 2, the child is able to symbolically represent objects and events, and internally (through representation) arrive at solutions to sensori-motor problems. The schemata of the 2-year-old are qualitatively and quantitatively superior to those of the younger child.

During the preoperational period (2 to 7 years) intellectual behavior moves from the sensori-motor level to the conceptual level. There is rapid language development that accompanies the rapid conceptual development of the period. During the period the child's thought is egocentric, the child being unable to assume the viewpoints of others and believing everything he thinks is "right." In conservation problems he is unaware of transformations of states and tends to "center" on perceptual aspects of problems. Thought by age 7 is pre-logical.

The concrete operational child (7 to 11 years) develops the use of logical thought. By the end of the period he can solve the conservation problems and most "concrete" problems. During these years the logical operations of reversibility, seriation, and classification are developed. The child can think logically, but he cannot apply his logic to verbal and hypothetical problems.

During the period of formal operations (11 to 15 years) cognitive structures (schemata) become qualitatively "mature." The child becomes structurally able to apply logical operations to all classes of problems. He can apply his logical thought to complex verbal problems, hypothetical problems, and problems involving the future. The child with formal operations can operate on an argument independent of its content. Logic becomes firmly available to the child as a tool of thought. During adolescence, formal thought is egocentric. The adolescent tries to reduce human behavior to what is logical and has difficulty coordinating his ideals with what is real.

At each new level of cognitive development, previous levels are incorporated and integrated. The preoperational child does not throw away his sensori-motor schemata and take up new ones. Sensori-motor schemata are modified and improved. The processes of assimilation and accommodation permit the continuous development of cognitive structures. Schemata are continually being modified throughout life, from birth throughout adulthood. While qualitative changes in cognitive structure cease after the development of formal operations, qualitative changes in content and function of intelligence continue.

Thus, early sensori-motor development is the foundation upon which later conceptual development is built. The basic paradigm of cognitive development for Piaget is seen as the assimilation and accommodation of experience, resulting in qualitative structural changes in cognitive machinery (schemata). In this sense, the child is truly father of the man.

Intelligence and Adaptation

For Piaget cognitive development is the intellectual counterpart of biological adaptation to the environment. As we adapt biologically to our environment, so too do we adapt intellectually. Through assimilation and accommodation the external world is organized and given structure. Schemata are the products of the organization.

Adaptation begins at birth with the exercise of sensori-motor reflexes. Differentiations via reflexes (sucking) are the first adaptations that are of eventual importance in cognitive development. As the child develops, the adaptations he makes are increasingly less related to sensory and motor behaviors alone, and may be less clearly seen as adaptations to the untrained eye.

Variables in Cognitive Development

The critical variables in cognitive development are: maturation, experience, social interaction, and equilibration. Piaget uses these terms in a general, not specific, way. He avoids the fruitless nature-nurture argument, whether intelligence is inherited (maturation) or learned (experience) by maintaining that each of the above variables is necessary for cognitive development but that none alone is sufficient to assure its occurrence. According to Piaget, the interaction of all four sets the course of development.

Two of the variables, maturation and equilibration, are not subject to any type of external control. The other two variables, experience and social interaction, are in part determined by external events. Experiential and social situations can be structured so the child can act upon things and interact with others. Piaget recognizes the potential effect of the "right" experience at the "right" time. While such structuring can be done, whether or not these experiences are assimilated and accommodated is still controlled by equilibration, an internal process.

There have been very few studies directed at validating Piagetian concepts of social interaction as a factor in cognitive development. The bulk of Piagetian studies have been concerned with experience as a variable. In these studies, social class, culture, and schooling have been found to be important variables. Several studies have found moderate correlations between social class and performance on Piaget-type tasks. A study by the author (Wadsworth, 1968) found social class to be related to performance on conservation tasks in kindergarten, but not to whether students learned to conserve during the study. The suggestion was that lower-class children attain conservation concepts at a slower rate than middle-class children, but that when levels of development are equated, there is no difference in acquisition.

The question of whether schooling can affect structural development is an important one. Few would argue that schooling does not affect cognitive content and function. Regarding structure, most studies conclude that children attain concrete operations about age 6 or 7 regardless of whether there has been formal schooling. A number of studies report the development of formal operations much more related to schooling. Mermelstein and Schulman (1967) found no difference between schooled and unschooled children in acquisition of conservation skills (concrete operations). Sigel and Mermelstein (1965) similarly found no difference on conservation tasks, but they did find a difference in favor of schooled children on class inclusion tasks (formal operations). Goodnow and Bethon (1966) found no difference on conservation tasks, but they found schooling was related to learning tasks requiring combinatorial reasoning. Thus, it would seem that the importance of schooling in developing cognitive structures *may be* most important in later than earlier periods. This question requires much more research.

Knowledge and Reality: a Construction

The developing child's knowledge of the world (and reality) is not a copy of the "objective" world. Each individual over the course of his development constructs knowledge and reality (through assimilation and accommodation). Knowledge is not transmitted directly but is constructed. Piaget (1967) writes:

The clearest result of our research on the psychology of intelligence is that even the structures most necessary to the adult mind, such as the logico-mathematical structures, are not innate in the child; they are built up little by little . . . There are no innate structures: every structure presupposes a construction. All these constructions originate from prior structures and revert, in the final analysis, . . . to the biological problem [p. 149-150].

Thus the development of cognitive structures and knowledge is an evolutionary process that takes place within every individual. The change is manifest in the individual's schemata which are constantly undergoing change. The process of assimilation ensures that schemata will not be copies of reality; accommodation ensures that constructions will have a measure of correspondence to the real world (Elkind, 1969, p. 329).

IMPLICATIONS OF PIAGET'S THEORY FOR EDUCATION

The remainder of this chapter deals with what the author feels are some of the clearer implications of Piaget's theory for educational practice. It must be kept in mind that Piaget has not directed his efforts toward the solution of educational problems. Clearly he has said much that is relevant to education. The application of his theory to educational practice requires that it be translated into applied settings. Obviously this requires considerable familiarity with the theory, much more than has been presented here. The implications suggested here are more general than specific.

Invariance of Concept Acquisition: When to Teach

Piaget's work states that cognitive structures (schemata) are developed in an invariant sequence. That is, the course of cognitive development, marked by the development of structures, is the same for all children, although the ages at which they attain particular structures may vary with intelligence and the social environment (Piaget and Inhelder, 1969, p. 153). Invariance was most clearly described in this work in the discussions of sensori-motor intelligence (Chapter Four) and the attainment of conservation skills (Chapters Four and Five). Research on the invariance concept, while not conclusive, tends to support Piaget's belief that acqusition of concepts is hierarchical and integrative in nature.

A word of caution. Piaget does not say that the sequence of cognitive development he describes is the only sequence in which schemata can be acquired. Piaget has described cognitive development, not determined how it *must* proceed. He does not preclude other possible sequences, though any other sequence would have to meet criteria that successive structures incorporate previous structures in an integrative and hierarchical fashion.

Assuming that concept acquisition is invariant, at least in Western cultures, then it makes educational sense to use Piaget's model of invariance in determining when to teach what. Curriculum sequences should be designed with children's changing cognitive status in mind. If curriculums do not take into account children's levels of conceptual development, learning is going to be inefficient. Children will not learn (develop schemata) if they do not have the prerequisite cognitive skills.

Readiness to learn is of particular concern to educators of elementary school children, though it should be of concern at all levels of education. According to Piagetian theory, a child is "ready" to develop a particular concept when, and only when, he has acquired the schemata that are necessary (prerequisites).

Individual Differences

Piaget has concerned himself primarily with the general psychological processes in cognitive development. He has not directly concerned himself with the topic of individual differences, though the fact that differences between individuals do exist is implicit in all his work. The major factor in cognitive development is the interaction of maturation, experience, social interactions, and equilibration. Clearly, different individuals can be expected to differ with respect to each of these variables.

Since development can be traced back to biological factors before birth, there can clearly be inherited biological differences affecting cognitive development. These can be manifest in different rates of *maturation* of relevant physiological structures.

Experience is a second variable in development. No two children have the same experiences. The history of experiences is different for every human being. Even identical twins raised in the same home cannot be assumed to have had the "same" experiences. Accordingly, differences in prior experiences can contribute to "individual differences" in cognitive development.

As children have different histories of general experiences, so do they have different histories of social experiences or *social interaction*. Because social interaction does not become an effective variable in cognitive development until after the egocentrism of the preoperational period comes to rest, the value of interactions prior to that time is as experience, not as social interaction. After age 6 or 7 interactions assume their "social" value. Clearly one's history of interactions, whether they are as experience or social, vary from person to person contributing to individual differences.

Equilibration is conceptualized as the regulator of the relationship between assimilation and accommodation. It can be thought of as a mode or style of regulation. A given event may be assimilated or accommodated differently by different persons. Many factors can contribute to this source of individual differences.

Children can be expected to differ in their histories of maturation, experience, social interaction, and equilibration, and they can differ in how these factors interact to govern cognitive development. The clear implication is that wide individual differences in conceptual development can be expected in children.

Methods of Assessing Conceptual Development

Methods of assessing the levels of conceptual development of children with respect to Piagetian concepts are needed. The Piagetian tasks can be used for diagnostic purposes to make such an assessment. Such a test of conceptual development (intelligence) is currently being developed at the University of Montreal by Adrien Pinard and Monique Laurendeau (1964). The test is being derived from Piaget's theory and represents an approach to test construction that is new. Conventional intelligence tests, such as the Stanford-Binet and the Wechsler scales, have been constructed by selecting items that reliably discriminate between chronological age groups. While these instruments are useful, a test such as the one being devised by Pinard should add an important dimension to assessing conceptual development.

Another method of assessing conceptual development, while derived from a different theoretical position than the one presented here, seems useful in the context of Piaget's theory and teacher requirements. Robert Gagné

124 Piaget's Theory of Cognitive Development

(1962, 1965) is an American educational psychologist concerned with learning. He is a behaviorist and thus approaches the question of learning from a different theoretical position than Piaget. What they do have in common is that they both conceptualize learning (concept acquisition) as taking place in a manner that is orderly, sequential, integrative, and hierarchical.

Gagné (1962, 1965) conceptualizes all learning as a function of prior learning, or prerequisite learnings. Learning of a particular concept only occurs if the concepts (or learnings) that are prerequisites to the concept have been acquired. Every bit of learning is thought of as generating a hierarchy in which prerequisite learnings can be identified (see Fig. 8). These prerequisites must be "learned" before the learning at the top of the hierarchy can occur. Gagné (1962) suggests hierarchies can be derived logically in certain content areas such as arithmetic and science. Hierarchies can be derived by beginning with a final learning task one is interested in and asking oneself the question: "What kind of capability would an individual have to possess if he were able to perform this task successfully, were we to give him only instructions?" (p. 356). Through systematic analysis, hierarchies of learnings can be derived in which lower members in the hierarchy serve as prerequisite learnings to higher members and all serve as prerequisites to the final learning. Experimental testing of such logically derived hierarchies have yielded predictable results (Gagné, 1962).

The similarity in Gagné's and Piaget's writings is that they both, in some respects, yield similar and useful ways for conceptualizing learning and for determining the level at which children can learn. They both see knowledge as accumulating in an orderly, sequential, and hierarchical manner. Both suggest there is an invariant order in which concepts may successfully be acquired.

Figure 8
Hypothetical Hierarchy of
Prerequisite Learnings

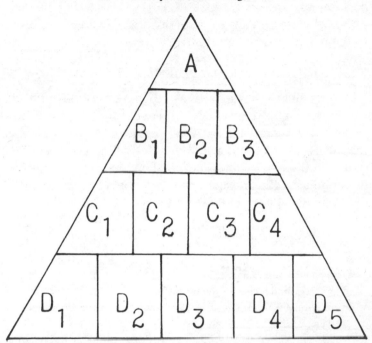

Since the writer has taken the liberty of suggesting that a behaviorist and developmentalist have something in common, it is important to indicate their main differences. Probably the most crucial point is with respect to the importance of "experience" in learning. According to Piaget, the organization of experience occurs within the organism (assimilation and accommodation) and the organism gives structure to experience. Thus, since organization is an internal process, external organization, such as the logical sequencing of learning experiences, cannot ensure internal organization. Gagné's position is that external organization is a necessary condition to optimize learning. The cognitive position assumes organization lies within the individual. The behaviorist position assumes organization is external to the individual.

Teaching Methods and Materials: How to Teach

Piaget's theory suggests that teaching methods and materials should be consistent with children's levels of conceptual development. *Active interactions* of the child with the environment (physical and social interactions) are seen as the most important school-related factor in cognitive development. Regarding school experiences and cognitive development, Piaget (1964) writes:

> Experience is always necessary for intellectual development ... but I fear that we may fall into the illusion that being submitted to an experience (a demonstration) is sufficient for a subject to disengage the structure involved. But more than this is required. The subject must be active, must transform things, and find the structure of his own actions on the objects [p. 4].

Cognitive reorganization resulting from assimilation and accommodation can only come about through the actions of the child. Thus actions, physical or cognitive, must occur if cognitive reorganization is going to take place. It must also be remembered that, according to Piaget, assimilation and accommodation of actions are always under internal control (equilibration) and reorganization of cognitive structures in a particular way can never be *ensured* by external organization of experience. A child's reorganization is always his own.

Through the period of concrete operations, manipulation of objects and materials dealing with concepts to be learned is most important. Seriation schemata (A < B, B < C thus A < C) can best be developed in concrete operational children if they visually and manually manipulate objects employing the concepts to be learned. In a similar manner, equivalence concepts (A = B, B = C, thus A = C) can best be learned if the child acts on objects that employ the concept. Reversibility in mathematical operations can be facilitated in children's learning if problems in multiplication and division are placed in opposition to one another (14 × 3_____; 42 ÷ 3_____; 42 ÷ 14_____). The same principle holds true for reversibility learnings in simple addition and subtraction. Problems placed in opposition demonstrate reversibility and help facilitate accommodation to the concept (5 + 4_____; 9 − 4_____; 9 − 5_____). Through the concrete operational period, concrete experiences generate conceptual development.

With the attainment of formal operations, children become able to develop concepts without the aid of direct physical experience. At this level, the activity of the child can be purely representational and independent of any "concrete" experience. The child can act on verbally presented conceptual material. Conceptual development can proceed based on the child's actions on written and verbal materials.

Social Interactions with Peers

Peer interactions become important with respect to cognitive development when the child becomes able to assimilate the viewpoints of others when they are different from his own. This comes about when the egocentrism of preoperational thought is dispelled around age 6 or 7. Accordingly, peer interactions are of cognitive importance from the time the child enters school. Children learn to evaluate their egocentric thoughts by comparing them to the thoughts of others. About the age of 6 or 7 most children become able to accommodate to the views of others. Thus peer interactions can be a fruitful means of stimulating natural cognitive conflicts that can generate accommodation to the views of others and evaluation of one's own concepts.

All types of situations in school that involve peer interactions are legitimate: role-playing, games, play, etc. They all stimulate peer interaction. Interactions can be centered on pertinent concepts. Conceptual development can be facilitated by making use of peer activities.

Sensori-Motor Development and Later Cognitive Development

Development resulting from motor and sensory behavior during the first two years of life is the bedrock upon which later cognitive development is built. The ability to represent objects symbolically develops from the reflex activities of the infant. Under "normal" conditions the child's actions in the environment ensure adequate development during the sensori-motor period and prepare the child for preoperational development. But this is not always the case. Development during the first two years of life can be impaired and affect later development.

The use of Piagetian concepts of sensori-motor development as they pertain to education and learning are reflected best in the work of Newell Kephart. Kephart is a clinician who is primarily interested in learning problems that can be traced to faulty learning in early childhood and how these problems can be corrected. Kephart has evolved, independently of Piaget, a diagnostic and remedial program for children with severe, non-physiological learning problems that in practice closely parallels Piaget's theory with respect to sensori-motor development. Kephart's views are most comprehensively dealt with in his book, *The Slow Learner in the Classroom* (1960), and are outlined elsewhere (Kephart, 1964). According to Kephart (Ibid.) the child's first interactions with his environment are motor; his first learnings and attempts to organize the environment are based on these motor interactions. Learning difficulty can begin during the motor stage if the child develops limited motor *skills* instead of general motor *patterns*. A motor skill is a specific motor act, such as walking, which is limited in application. The motor skill of walking permits the young child to place one foot in front of the other, but it may not permit him to solve problems in walking, such as getting around objects. A motor pattern of walking is more generalized and useful in solving motor problems. Only through the development of motor patterns does the child develop a stable body of motor information about his environment.

With the development of a number of motor patterns, such as locomotion, manipulation, balance, throwing and catching, the child evolves a stable body of useful information about his environment. The initial information is motor. Information processing is on a motor level. For further progress, the child's system of motor knowledge must be transferred to objects in his environment that he cannot touch and manipulate. Since he cannot investigate these objects in a motor fashion, he must learn to investigate perceptually. At this point though, perceptual data (obtained through vision and hearing) are not organized as motor data are organized. Perceptual data come to be organized by projecting motor organization onto perceptual data.

The transfer of the structure of motor data to perceptual data is called the "perceptual-motor match" by Kephart.

Concepts useful to the child are initially motor. When motor patterns become stable, the child can begin to transfer the motor organization. As the child manipulates objects and receives motor data, he also watches the manipulation and receives unstructured visual data. Exploration with the eyes duplicates exploration with the hands. As the child repeatedly receives structured motor data and unstructured visual data, the visual data comes to take on the structure of the motor data through the perceptual-motor match. When the visual data become structured in the same way as the motor data (after the perceptual-motor match is complete) then, and only then, do visual data have enough structure to adequately evaluate events in the environment. Unlike motor evaluations, perceptual evaluations can be made of all objects and events that can be perceived. Distant objects can be construed as well as those close at hand.

According to Kephart, inadequacies in development can occur at several points. Children may fail to develop initial motor patterns from which useful perceptual patterns may be transferred. Second, the perceptual-motor match may not occur or may not be completed. If this happens, the child will have problems developing a stable and useful perceptual world. For example, suppose a child does not develop a motor pattern of the spatial relationships of "up," "down" and "right," "left." He cannot then transfer the motor relationship to perceptual data and may not develop stable perceptual awarenesses of the relationships. He may not be able to "see" the difference between up and down and right and left. This might not become evident until the child enters school and receives reading instruction. A child developing as described may be unable to "see" the difference between "b" and "p," or between "d" and "q," or between "M" and "W." These pairs of letters may look alike to the child and make learning how to read rather difficult.

According to Kephart's formulation, an inability to differentiate between letters (shapes) may be traced to faulty learning during motor development. The number of different problems of the type that have been described are innumerable. Both Piaget and Kephart agree that people "learn" to perceive (see and hear). Learning can be faulty or inefficient and may require correction. It is unfortunate that many of the symptoms of faulty early learning do not show up until the child is in second or third grade. Also, many children may be inappropriately labeled brain damaged, dyslexic, perceptually handicapped, or retarded (or a host of other names that all smack of organic impairment) when the real problem is a matter of motor or perceptual learning.

Under normal conditions the child's environment presents him with enough situations requiring him to make enough accommodations to ensure adequate perceptual and motor development. When deficits do occur, specific remediation is required. Specific suggestions for dealing with specific perceptual-motor learning problems are provided by Kephart in *The Slow Learner in the Classroom* (1960), and in *Steps to Achievement for the Slow Learner* (1968), as well as a number of other of his works.

Educational Intervention and Piaget

There is great concern in educational circles as to whether educational intervention offers a solution to the problems of the "disadvantaged" and other deprived groups of children. Can conceptual development be speeded up? Can early intervention (preschool) compensate for social class differences in academic "readiness"? Piaget's theory of cognitive development does not provide a clear answer to these questions. Development is a function of the interaction of maturation, experience, social interaction, and equilibration. Presumably, within the limitations of maturation and equilibration, experiences (both social and general) can be manipulated. This does not ensure the child will act on the elements in a situation and assimilate and accommodate according to a formula. Piaget does not say how or under what specific conditions conceptual development can be advanced. In addition, the consequences of advancing development are not clear. Unfortunately for education, Piaget has been concerned with how concepts develop and not how to develop concepts.

Several authorities on Piaget's work suggest early intervention may not be fruitful. Elkind (1969) writes:

> ... the Piagetian conception of intelligence provides no support either for those who advocate formal preschool instruction or for those who argue for new methods and materials to stimulate intrinsic motivation [p. 335].

Comments by Kohlberg (1968) are only slightly more encouraging:

> I have claimed that a Piagetian conception of methods of accelerating intellectual development (employing cognitive conflict, match, and sequential ordering of experience), a Piagetian focus upon basic intellectual operations, and a Piagetian procedure of assessment of general intellectual development might generate somewhat more general and long-range cognitive effects than would other approaches.
>
> Basically, however, the Piaget approach does not generate great optimism as to the possibility of preschool acceleration of cognitive development (or of compensation for its retardation) nor does it lead to a rationale in which such acceleration (or compensation) is especially critical during the preschool years [p. 1056].

A LAST WORD

As an educational psychologist, the writer feels one of the most important determinants of teachers' behaviors with respect to students is how they (the teachers) conceptualize phenomena. The classic example can be seen in the nature-nurture controversy that has pervaded psychology for years. If a teacher conceptualizes intelligence (the ability to succeed in school) as "fixed," she (or he) is probably not going to be motivated to try very hard to help a student who is a poor performer in the classroom. On the other hand, a teacher who conceptualizes intelligence as "developed," not fixed, may be motivated to help the poor performer. How teachers conceptualize intelligence and learning will influence their actions. Teachers' expectations of how children can perform in the classroom are derived from their conceptualizations. The fact that teacher expectations (as well as parental expectation and self-expectation) are communicated to students and affect their achievement has been well documented (Rosenthal and Jacobsen, 1968). How teachers conceptualize will have a lot to do with how much is learned, and who learns, in their classrooms.

The writer believes Piaget's conceptualizations (theory) are a set that are at once comprehensive and useful. They offer an alternative way of conceptualizing behavior and development for those interested in psychology and education. At best, psychology as a science operates on the level of theories. There are no laws in psychology (as in physics or chemistry), so one must be content with using theories and try to find those that are most useful. All theories in psychology are constantly changing, being validated, tested, and reorganized. To ask if a theory is "right" or "wrong" is a poor question. Some theories are useful for explaining one phenomenon and useless for explaining another. Thus the user of theories (and conceptualizations) must pick and choose with care. Generally, acceptance or rejection of a theory is a function of its utility in predicting behavior, its persuasive power, its logic, and its novelty. All these criteria reflect the appeal of Piaget's work.

There is little doubt that Piaget's theory of cognitive development will continue to change and become more refined, as it has over the years. Some of his concepts may not stand up in the face of future research. Others certainly will. The writer has presented a look at the part of Piaget's conceptualizations that seem to be most important for education. Needless to say, the implications of Piaget's concepts for education have not been exhausted in this work. The author's interpretations of Piaget's writings have produced some implications that are very general in nature. They are not remedies for educational problems. They are a start. Piaget's work over the last fifty years has generated a degree of interest and inquiry that is unprecedented and shall continue for many years. The writer hopes an interest in Piaget's concepts has been generated here.

Bibliography

Ebersole, M., Kephart, N., and Ebersole, J., *Steps to Achievement for the Slow Learner*. Columbus: Charles E. Merrill, 1968.

Elkind, D. "Children's Discovery of the Conservation of Mass, Weight, and Volume: Piaget's Replication Study II." *Journal of Genetic Psychology* 98 (1961): 219-227.

____. "Quality Conceptions in Junior and Senior High School Students." *Child Development* 32 (1961): 551-560.

____. "Egocentrism in Adolescence." *Child Development* 38 (1967): 1025-1034.

____. "Cognitive Structures and Adolescent Experience." *Adolescence* 2 (1967-1968): 427-434.

____. "Giant in the Nursery." *The New York Times Magazine* (May 26, 1968), 25.

____. "Piagetian and psychometric conceptions of intelligence." *Harvard Educational Review* 39 (1969): 319-337.

Erickson, E. *Childhood and Society*. New York: W. W. Norton, 1950.

Flavell, J. *The Developmental Psychology of Jean Piaget*. Princeton, N. J.: D. Van Nostrand, 1963.

Freud, A. *The Ego and the Mechanisms of Defense*. New York: International Universities Press, 1946.

Gagné, R. M. "The Acquisition of Knowledge." *Psychological Review* 69 (1962): 355-365.

____. *The Conditions of Learning*. New York: Holt, Rinehart and Winston, 1965.

Goldschmid, M. L. "Different Types of Conservation and Nonconservation and Their Relation to Age, Sex, I.Q., M.A., and Vocabulary." *Child Development* 38 (1967): 1229-1246.

Goodnow, J., and Bethon, G. "Piaget's Tasks: The Effects of Schooling and Intelligence." *Child Development* 37 (1966): 573-582.

Greenfield, P. M. "On Culture and Conservation." In *Studies in Cognitive Growth* edited by J. Bruner, *et al.* New York: Wiley, 1966.

Gruen, G. E. "Experiences Affecting the Development of Number Conservation in Children." *Child Development* 36 (1965): 964-979.

Hooper, I. H. "Piagetian Research and Education." In *Logical Thinking in Children* edited by I. E. Sigel and F. H. Hooper, pp. 423-434. New York: Holt, Rinehart and Winston, 1968.

Hunt, J. McV. *Intelligence and Experience*. New York: Ronald Press, 1961.

Inhelder, B., and Piaget, J. *The Growth of Logical Thinking from Childhood to Adolescence*, translated by Anne Parsons and Stanley Pilgram. New York: Basic Books, 1958.

____. *The Early Growth of Logic in the Child*. London: Routledge and Kegan Paul, 1964.

Kephart, N. C. *The Slow Learner in the Classroom*. Columbus: Charles E. Merrill, 1960.

____. "Perceptual-Motor Aspects of Learning Disabilities." *Exceptional Children* 31 (1964): 201-206.

Kohlberg, L. "The Montessori Approach to Cultural Deprivation. A Cognitive Development Interpretation and Some Research Findings." In *Preschool Education, Theory, Research, and Action*, edited by R. Hess and R. Bear. Chicago: Aldine, 1968.

____. "Early Education: A Cognitive-Developmental View." *Child Development* 39 (1968): 1013-1063.

L'Abate, L. "Frequency of Citation Study in Child Psychology Literature." *Child Development* 40 (1968): 87-92.

Mermelstein, E., and Schulman, L. "Lack of Formal Schooling and the Acquisition of Conservation." *Child Development* 38 (1967): 39-52.

Piaget, J. *The Language and Thought of the Child*. New York: Harcourt, Brace and World, 1926.

____. *Judgment and Reasoning of the Child*. New York: Harcourt, Brace and World, 1928.

____. *The Child's Conception of Physical Causality*. New York: Harcourt, Brace and World, 1930.

____. *The Moral Judgment of the Child*. New York: Harcourt, Brace and World, 1932.

____. *The Child's Conception of Number*. London: Humanities Press, 1952.

____. "Autobiography." In *History of Psychology in Autobiography* edited by E. G. Boring, *et al.*, pp. 237-256. 4 vols. Worcester, Mass.: Clark University Press, 1952.

____. *The Origins of Intelligence in Children*. New York: International Universities Press, 1952.

____. *The Construction of Reality in the Child*, translated by Margaret Cook. New York: Basic Books, 1954.

____. "The Genetic Approach to the Psychology of Thought." *Journal of Educational Psychology* 52 (1961): 275-281.

____. *Play, Dreams and Imitation in Childhood*. New York: W. W. Norton, 1962.

____. *The Child's Conception of the World*. Paterson, N. J.: Littlefield, Adams, 1963.

____ *The Psychology of Intelligence*. Paterson, N. J.: Littlefield, Adams, 1963.

____. "Three Lectures." In *Piaget Rediscovered*, edited by R. E. Ripple and U. N. Rockcastle. Ithaca, N. Y.: Cornell University Press, 1964.

____. *Six Psychological Studies*. New York: Vintage Books, 1967.

____. *The Mechanisms of Perception*. New York: Basic Books, 1969.

____. *Genetic Epistemology*. New York: Columbia University Press, 1970.

Piaget, J., and Inhelder, B. *The Child's Conception of Space*. London: Routledge and Kegan Paul, 1956.

____. *The Psychology of the Child*, translated by Helen Weaver. New York: Basic Books, 1969.

Piaget, J., Inhelder, B., and Szeminska, A. *The Child's Conception of Geometry*. New York: Basic Books, 1960.

Pinard, A., and Laurendeau, M. "A Scale of Mental Development Based on the Theory of Piaget: Description of a Project." *Journal of Research in Science Teaching*, 2 (1964): 253-260.

Rosenthal, R., and Jacobson, L. *Pygmalion in the Classroom*. New York: Holt, Rinehart and Winston, 1968.

Sigel, I. E. "The Attainment of Concepts." In *Review of Child De-*

velopment Research, edited by M. L. Hoffman and L. V. Hoffman. New York: Russell Sage Foundation, 1964, vol. 1, pp. 209-248.

Sigel, E. E., and Hooper, F. H. *Logical Thinking in Children: Research Based on Piaget's Theory*. New York: Holt, Rinehart and Winston, 1968.

Smedslund, J. "The Acquisition of Conservation of Substance and Weight in Children." In *Readings in Child Development and Behavior*, edited by G. Stendler. New York: Harcourt, Brace and World, 1964.

Uzgiris, I. "Situational Generality of Conservation." In *Logical Thinking in Children*, edited by I. E. Sigel and F. H. Hooper, pp. 40-52. New York: Holt, Rinehart and Winston, 1968.

Wadsworth, B. "The Effect of Peer Group Social Interaction on the Conservation of Number Learning in Kindergarten Children," unpublished Ed.D. dissertation, State University of New York at Albany, 1968.

Wallach, L., Wall, J., and Anderson, L. "Number Conservation: The Roles of Reversibility, Addition, Subtraction, and Misleading Perceptual Cues." *Child Development* 38 (1967): 425-442.

Wohlwill, J., and Lowe, R. "Experimental Analysis of the Development of Conservation of Number." *Child Development* 33 (1962): 153-168.

Zimiles, H. "The Development of Differentiation and Conservation of Number." *Monograph Society for Research in Child Development* 31 (1966).

Index